REFUSING
QUIT
to

be good. do good. always.

[signature]

REFUSING
QUIT *to*

AMAZING LIFE STORIES ABOUT TRANSFORMING ADVERSITY INTO VICTORY

Napoleon Hill Foundation Instructors and Students

A publication of
Compass Mastermind

ISBN: 1518826245
ISBN 13: 9781518826245
Library of Congress Control Number: 2015918045
CreateSpace Independent Publishing Platform
North Charleston, South Carolina

Published By:

Compass Mastermind

Website: www.compassmastermind.com
Email: success@compassmastermind.com

Written by:

Napoleon Hill Foundation Instructors and Students

DEDICATION PAGE

Dedicated to everyone who is pursuing a life of purpose to benefit others despite the challenges they encounter.

ACKNOWLEDGMENTS

WE ARE EXTREMELY thankful for each other's chapter contribution and support given to our book *"Refusing to Quit"*. The following individuals who without sharing their inspiring stories this collaborative book would not have been written: Alexander Alfaro, Codruta Bala, Michelle Casey, Tim Chhim, John Westley Clayton, Tom Cunningham, Brenda Dear, Sandra Ruiz-Desai, Chuck DeWayne, Dave Doyle, Colin Gilmartin, Tami Jackson, Eduard Lopez, Shannon McVagh, Ruth Neslo, Aristoteles Nielsen, Marianne Noad, Ore Ohimor, Christy Onabu, Jeremy Rayzor, Samuel Standley, Taylor Tagg, Takeshi Umemura, Hillary Vargas, Vayu Yamada, and Shadiya Zackaria.

We are thankful for our editors Tom Cunningham and Cheryl Long for their time and efforts to make our chapters the best they can be.

We want to share our warmest gratitude for the completion of this project through the guidance and positive encouragement from Tom Cunningham, Colin Gilmartin, Janet Jones, John Westley Clayton, Taylor Tagg, and Jeremy Rayzor.

We thank Don M. Green (Executive Director), the entire Board of Trustees and staff from The Napoleon Hill Foundation for their unconditional persistence to perpetuate Napoleon Hill's success philosophy.

We offer our sincere appreciation to Judy Williamson (Director), Uriel "Chino" Martinez, and Alan Chen for the learning opportunities provided by Napoleon Hill World Learning Center. Without the existence of the World Learning Center most of us would not have had the privilege of becoming friends and learning from the many beneficial services that it provides.

We all appreciate the unwavering moral and emotional support of our respective family and friends. You were also part of this project even though you may not have been aware of the support that you have given us; it started before this book project.

Above all, utmost appreciation to Dr. Napoleon Hill who dedicated his life to positively inspire countless millions of people in the past, present, and future generations to live a better life.

-Compass Mastermind

TESTIMONIALS

"REFUSING TO QUIT" takes the message and expands it into the lives of successful Napoleon Hill Instructors and Students for the benefit of today's readers. I highly recommend this book to help you understand the importance of the don't quit philosophy on your success journey."

-Don Green,
Executive Director of The Napoleon Hill Foundation

Refusing to Quit is not just a book title. It's a directive. The examples provided inside these pages will inspire you to keep going and keep moving forward regardless of obstacles, both physical and mental. The people who have written this book are messengers of meaning and opportunity. Your job as reader is to take advantage of these messages so that you may succeed beyond your expectations.

-Jeffrey Gitomer
Author of The Little Red Book of Selling and YES! Attitude

"Since I first discovered Napoleon Hill's work more than 20 years ago, his words and principles have profoundly impacted the direction and quality of my life. The thought-provoking, personal stories in this book reminded me that each one of us is capable of incredible things when we never give up on our dreams. "

- Ken Honda
Best Selling Author of Self-Development Books in Japan

Wow, what a fantastic Book! I LOVED it. "Refusing to Quit" is a Powerful book.

Going through Adversity in business and having a devastating life changing accident that left me Dis-Abled and an Amputee, I have become an expert at "Refusing to Quit." Being friends with Zig Ziglar over 20 years I can tell you Zig had that same "Refusing to Quit " attitude. So much of Zigs influence was from Napoleon Hill, learning philosophies and principles that would guide Zig and that he would pass on down to thousands of people and I have been privileged to be one of those.

Pick up this book, read and absorb a chapter a day and you to will learn from those same principles and philosophies that helped me and so many thousands of us to become successful at overcoming Adversity and "Refusing to Quit"

Have a Fantastic Day!

-Phillip Hatfield
The TRANSFORMER
Zig Ziglar company speaker and author

In "Refusing to Quit", I have noticed that the common denominator remains the great book of Dr. Napoleon Hill's: Think & Grow Rich – which is also the center of gravitation of Napoleon Hill's writings...Therefore,

I will suggest that the contributing authors, who are the Napoleon Hill's Disciples should continue to spread the gospel – that for people to have peace of mind and to key in to the super highways of accurate thinking; one must practice and immerse oneself with the principles in the book; especially the Six Steps that Turned Desire into Gold - because that is where you will derive 98% of the secrets of Napoleon Hill's writings...Indeed, having been following Napoleon Hill's writings for the past 37years – as well as the fact that the said chapter also contributed over 95% of what I had achieved in life!...Thus, I recommend this book for everybody's reading!

-Poly I. Emenike, BSc, MSc (Lagos); OPM (HARVARD); Ph.D.(ISM.) Author of three books: Entrepreneurial Spirits... The Benefits of Adventures; and How To Alter Your Destiny To The Direction You Want...Napoleon Hill Foundation Gold Award Winner, 2012; Napoleon Hill Foundation representative in Africa; Honorary member Board of Trustee of Napoleon Hill Foundation; a certify instructor of Napoleon Hill Success Principles and Nigeria National Honors Award Winner in 2011.

"I have said this to many people who I have met over the years. Almost always the worst things that have happened to me ended up giving birth to the best things in my life. So I personally look at challenges as opportunities. I get excited about challenges. So this book and the stories within it resonate with me at a deep level. Great job for using your failure as the opportunity to discover yourself and find your life's purpose! And great job for a book well done."

-Naren Arulrajah
Founder, CEO, ekwa.com

What an amazing book! You get 26 different guaranteed ways to win. Each instructor pours into you the absolute meaning of "Refusing To Quit". Being an author, "The Rod Effect" and a former professional football player I know this all too well. Winning is the only option and you will find that magic within these pages.

-Rod Smith
Former wide receiver of the Denver Broncos
2 time Super Bowl winner and 3 Pro Bowl appearances

"Refusing to Quit" is a very inspiring book with true-life stories of people in the present world who have fought life's adversities to emerge victorious. It contains powerful stories about courage, determination, persistence and principle centered living. It's all about people who refused to quit, determined to live life on their own terms despite roadblocks and failure on the way. These stories of success reflect universal principles that can uplift anybody's life no matter at which station in life they are. I thoroughly enjoyed reading these stories and recommend this book to everybody looking for inspiration to take their life to the next level from good to great. Congratulations for shining a light for people in your generation by finding the courage to fly high in your life. Wish you all success as you forge ahead towards greater accomplishment by refusing to quit in the face of adversity."

-Aslam Shaikh
Managing Director/CEO
Realty Property Development (Pvt) Limited

Throughout my business life, I met many successful people from all walks of life. One of my greatest blessings was having Napoleon Hill work for me. Throughout our many conversations, including several overnight stays at our home, Hill shared his Success Principles with me. His most common advice and admonition were to persist until you reach your goal. This book, "Refusing To Quit", written by 26 Napoleon Hill Foundation Certified Instructors and students, mirrors Hill's own business career.

If you like stories of people who have persisted until they reached their goals, and beyond, this is the book for you. It is Napoleon Hill's Success Principles for today's time.

-Ben Gay III
Author & Sales Trainer
The Closers

FORWARD

REFUSING TO QUIT is such an important topic that a distinguished group of followers of the Napoleon Hill success principles have compiled their stories on the subject in a most informative new book.

Chapters have been written by people who have distinguished themselves by studying Napoleon Hill to the degree that they have been certified as an instructor of the Napoleon Hill Foundation; students of Napoleon Hill have written other chapters. When you read "Think and Grow Rich", if you have not already done so, you will discover Napoleon Hill's first chapter contains stories with the "don't quit" message. Edwin Barnes' desire to work with Edison, R.U. Darby in Three Feet From Gold, The Strange Power of a child and Henry Ford's desire for a v-8 motor are all stories on persistence, don't quit instructions.

"Refusing to Quit" takes the message and expands it into the lives of successful Napoleon Hill Instructors and Students for the benefit of today's readers.

I highly recommend this book to help you understand the importance of the don't quit philosophy on your success journey.

Don Green
Executive Director
The Napoleon Hill Foundation

Introduction Page

Dear Friends of Napoleon Hill,

What a pleasure to see so many people come together in this book and discuss the value of Dr. Hill's Science of Success Philosophy in their lives. Surely, by reading this book, you will have many questions as to how and why you too can become involved. Questions from potential students that I hear almost daily are:

1) Why should I study this philosophy? It just seems to be just common sense.
2) What can this philosophy do for me if I decide to join the class?
3) Can you guarantee the results that I expect from the course?

Let's take a closer look at each of the three questions and then you can decide for yourself as to whether or not the courses would be of benefit to you personally.

Question 1: Dr. Hill's Philosophy is based on what the successful person does in achieving success. It is common sense but unfortunately as we have heard, common sense is not so common. Dr. Hill not only observed what successful people do, but created a success system after interviewing people for well over twenty years. Essentially you can say that he spent his lifetime doing case studies of successful people and then analyzed their performance and noted what major characteristics were held in common. Today, we have 17 principles of success that he concluded were the components of his findings. You may know some or all, but the beauty in the system is how they merge together to create a unity of effort that puts a person on Dr. Hill's "success beam." In class, each student is asked to examine his or her active use of the principles, and thereby determine how closely they measure up to the standard or go beyond. This comparison is an indicator in itself of how close you are to rubbing shoulders with success.

Question 2: If you decide to study Dr. Hill's success philosophy, results are based upon the effort that you put into your own performance. There is no guarantee that you will achieve anything simply by enrolling in the class and paying your tuition. Education is an inside job. If you put in the effort consistent with your goal, you will receive the results you are anticipating. However, you must do the homework first prior to achieving any type of outcome. It is the action on your part that guarantees your degree of success. Dedicated time, consistent effort, and attitude of service are the three ingredients for positive outcomes. There are no shortcuts, detours, or instantaneous results. It takes time, but the end results are worth it if you stick with the process.

Question 3: You are the only person who can predetermine your results. It is self-discipline, persistence, and consistency of effort over time -- your effort -- that forecasts good results. Not the class, not the teacher, and not the curriculum, but YOU. The course is simply a vehicle to guide you where you want to go. As a car gets you to your destination, so too this system of study will transport you to a whole new way of seeing and achieving success.

Given the above considerations, it is now a good idea to read the stories and testimonials contained in the following chapters. Each person is giving an individual account as to why Dr. Hill's philosophy has been advantageous to them. All are different and unique, but each shares a commonality with the others and that is that all the writers in this book have learned and benefitted from studying Dr. Hill. His is a philosophy for Everyman. From a GED to a Ph.D., people in all walks of life look at their performance through the lens of self-improvement. This introspection enables each student to become the person that he or she dreams about becoming.

If you are interested in taking a single class or studying to become a certified instructor, you can access information about the process by visiting our website at www.naphill.org. Once on the website you can learn about the curriculum and the three courses offered. Briefly, the courses are described below:

Step 1 is the Self Study Course that introduces students to Dr. Hill's philosophy. It is a guided study of the 17 success principles that you work through at your own pace.

Step 2 is the Internet Distance Learning Class that runs three times a year. In this course your work is supervised by an certified instructor. You receive personalized feedback. As a final project you complete an Action Plan that covers the next 3-5 years in your life. It is reviewed and commented upon by the instructor.

Step 3 is the Leader Certification Class that you must attend in person. Often it is offered 2-3 times a year both domestically in the USA and internationally at various sites around the world. This class requires your attendance in person, a comprehensive exam, a service project, and a videotape of you teaching a lesson.

Start to finish the three step process can be completed in a year, however, many people take longer depending upon their personal schedule.

Our courses attract students from around the world. Students from many countries may be in your classes and the end result is that you have worldwide friends, alliances, and mentors that can assist you greatly in your efforts to achieve success.

Take the time. Read this book. Devote yourself to study. Then decide if what is offered is for you. If so, log on to the www. naphill.org website, signup for the "Thought for the Day" and "weekly Ezine," and learn what it is all about.

Hope to see you in our very next course, and looking forward to meeting you in our next in-person class. In the meantime, be your very best always!

Judy Williamson
Director of Education
The Napoleon Hill Foundation

Table Of Contents

Three Warning Signs

By Tim Chhim

What would you do?

You have just turned 20 years of age and you have many more years to live in this beautiful world.

BUT – imagine this!

Imagine you are dropped in the middle of a deep jungle. The sky is dark and gloomy with drizzling rain dropping down on your frail and weak body.

You are sitting on soaking and nasty ground, which stinks like slushy mud in a pigsty. You are waiting in a long line for your name to be called. When you look around, many guards, with their AK 47 rifles are watching you like a hawk. They are ready to shoot you when you make any kind of wrong move. Nearly a hundred innocent people, including women and children, are waiting in the same line… and they most likely do not know what is going to happen to them next.

Imagine further that you know you have less than one hour to live! You are put in that long line waiting to be executed somewhere in the deep and dark jungle! Not to be shot by a firing squad …but to be clubbed with a bloodstained hoe.

Now, those people who are waiting in front of you are being called and taken away, one by one, into a deep jungle by the would be killers.

Imagine, finally, that you will be forced to dig your own grave and, when you are done, the butchers will tie both of your arms behind your back and tell you to kneel down facing your own grave… and in the end they will strike the back of your head forcing you to fall into the ditch... and the only life that you have, and treasure, will be over, and your dream to become a free man living in the freest country on earth will die with you.

WHAT WILL YOU DO? WHAT...WILL... YOU DO?

(Please - don't worry; smile instead, because you very likely in a nice and comfortable room, and you are about to read or listen to part of my real, and incredible story.

It began with a dream—Definiteness of purpose

When the United States' influence reached Cambodia in 1970, I also began to have a recurring dream, visualizing undoubtedly that one-day I would live as a free man.

I would become a free man mentally, spiritually and bodily. I would be free from being hunger, oppression, and in control of all aspects of my life. With my eyes closed, the pictures of freedom appeared...freedom to see, speak, listen, feel, and play, and moreover to pray, love and to live. That dream stuck in my mind for many years.

I gave over five years of my young and precious life to help fight for my dream. I was going to school during the day and carrying a gun by night-- the gun was much taller than I was. Hundreds of my schoolmates disappeared, or died, from the onslaught of the well-equipped communist Vietcong and the North Vietnamese forces, who invaded Cambodia to use its territories to fight the American forces in South Vietnam. Many more died from attacks of Vietnamese trained insurgents, known as the communist Khmer Rouge. I believed in the Americans, and had very high hopes that they would continue to help fight the communist until Cambodia won the war for freedom, as they had promised.

I DREAMED ON....

However, a few short years after the Americans stopped helping, my dream of being a free man disappeared. The communist Khmer

Rouge, the Vietnamese ally, won the war. They entered the Capital and forced millions of people, including me, my relatives, and my friends to flee our home by foot, without having enough food and supplies, to go to an unknown location. They told us that we could return in several days.

Among hundreds of thousands of people—the sick, the injured, the old, the pregnant, the young, and the babies in their mother's arm—the soldiers forced me, and my relatives, to leave our home by foot under the scorching April Sun, the hottest season in Cambodia.

For many days and nights, and many miles away from home, I slept on the dirty ground along the riverbank that, most of the time, I needed to hold my nose because of the foul odor of dead or decaying bodies nearby.

During those many long days, I had to walk, and jump over, hundreds of dead soldiers who were left lying on the sizzling blacktopped roadway. On both sides of the shoulders I could spot countless more freshly dead or decayed bodies that were still in a fighting position, with their guns and uniforms on. My heart jumped every time I heard my relatives waking up at night screaming from horrible nightmares.

TURNING FEAR INTO FAITH.

About two weeks after the expulsion, as food was extremely limited, water was dirty, and suffering from insect bites having heat stroke from drifting under the open sky, I became severely ill. Other people around me were also too sick, or died, without proper care.

I looked at my pale, wrinkled, and greasy skin - it was pale and yellow. I was trembling and feared that my life, like many others, was coming to an end. Yet, my faith, and dream for "freedom", was much stronger than my fear of death. I realized that my body was getting weaker and weaker, with excruciating pain all over; yet only my mind was getting stronger, along with my faith in life. I believed that freedom was waiting for me somewhere beyond the horizon.

My heart was also aching for Sopheap, a young woman whom I loved dearly. She and her family members were also forced to leave, and had been fleeing along highway 5 with my relatives and myself. I noticed that her asthma had gotten worse day by day. At the same time I was hoping that, in the end, she and I would have a bright future together.

For the next few days, walking one single step made me feel like I was dragging a ton of rock with my feet. What was left in me was only my spiritual belief in the highest power, that IT would help me save my life. I made it to the first check point, where the communist soldiers started screening everyone's background. Unfortunately, all evictees, who were by now looking like zombies, were told to go back to the place where their ancestors once lived. That was when my hope to be with Sopheap ended. Sadly, the road leading to our ancestor's homes were in the opposite direction.

THE TEAKETTLE:

The next day, on that rainy afternoon before we said goodbye, I sat with Sopheap under a jujube tree by an old teakettle, which we used to boil hot water to drink, to discuss our future. I asked her to come with me to the north where my ancestors lived. She went inside her makeshift tent and came back in tears. Her parents had totally rejected the idea and told her I had nothing to offer for her future. The only words I could say to her were my handwritten note that I engraved on the teakettle, "Goodbye! and I will always love you!" We went our different ways while hiding our tears with raindrops. I turned around many times to see her and finally her figure disappeared into the misty rain.

A few days later, the communist soldiers herded me, along with my relatives, to stay in several different uninhabited Buddhist temples, before abandoning us on an empty field with hundreds of other families to survive on our own and to wait for new instructions. By this time, most of my relatives had become sick from lack of food, water and medical treatment. We tried to build our temporary shack with small tree branches and hay, to protect us from rainfalls and the scorching sun.

THE LAST HAPPINESS

One early morning, several days later, the soldiers called out my name, and dozens of other pre-selected former government workers and their family members, and rounded us up for their next instructions. They told us that we would go back to the Capital to help rebuild the country and to welcome Cambodia's famous Prince Sihanouk. I was excited because I would be able to go back to living a normal life and, especially, to help rebuild the country. Several soldiers with guns herded us across many rice fields and along forests to another unspecified location to be brought to the Capital.

Everyone was cheerful and so was I. I could see their eyes glowing and their smiling face for the first time. We were walking happily in a long line behind the soldiers who kept on leading us forward. I was among the last people in the long row because I was still weak and could not keep up with the crowd. However, I was excited for the new opportunity and was hoping to see all my old friends including Sopheap.

THE FIRST MESSAGE

Somewhere in the wood, while we were still following the soldiers, a frail and half naked young man hysterically jumped in front of me from his nearby hideout, on his knees begging me on his not to talk out loud. My heart pounded. He looked me in the eyes and whispered that the soldiers were taking us to be executed—with a hoe –then they would dump us in a grave. He turned around and showed me a huge bloodstained gash behind his neck. He pleaded with me to escape, and begged me for some clothes. I gave him my t-shirt. He told me he knew me and I believed I also knew him. Yet still, I did not believe his story. I trusted the soldiers' words.

Hours later, the soldiers placed us in an old Buddhist temple and told us to campout anywhere on the temple's ground to wait for transportation crews. I didn't see any transport vehicle except an old GMC truck with flat tires parked nearby. The soldiers fed us with some boiling rice and assured us with their hourly speeches that we would be all right.

The Second Message

The next afternoon, while I was coming back from bathing in the pond behind the temple, I met a hunchbacked old man who brought dozens of cows to drink at the pond. After looking around the place suspiciously, the man asked me if I had a match or cigarette lighter. I told him I didn't smoke. He then asked me what I was doing at the temple. He pointed toward the mountains with his lips and quietly told me that he smelled a heavy stench from the mountains every time he was there to feed his cows. He complimented me on my pair of sandals. I offered him the sandals but he refused. He told me I would need them badly. He whispered that, on the national route, a few kilometers away, many evictees were still being led away to unknown places and I needed the sandals to protect my feet. He winked at me several times and left! I wondered why the man told me about the foul-smelling mountains and about the national route.

The Final Message

The night felt into a still and quiet darkness, except for the sound of dogs' barking, as the soldiers patrolled the temple grounds. I could not sleep well, mostly from being hungry and from thinking about what was going to happen to my dream for freedom. I found a place to snooze in a dilapidated monk's house, on a few broken wood panels. I thought about my friend, the young man with the bloody gash on the back of his head. Then I thought about the old man with the cows, who seemed to suggest that I leave that place. However, I still considered the government's promise, delivered every other hour, as reasonable... They asked us to be patient and to wait for the transportation. I felt comfortable that the government would not kill harmless citizens.

The long night came and went. I greeted the new sunrise with curiosity. I went out the west gate of the temple after hearing the morning speech by a Communist cadet. A frail woman, with long and uncombed salt and pepper hair, was sitting inside a small old shack under a huge tree near the gate. I walked toward her and greeted her kindly. Her face turned white as a ghost. She told me that the temple was used as encampment before people were being sent to the mountains. No one was ever transported away by truck. She then asked me if I had any clothes to trade for food, because she thought I was hungry. I told her to wait so I could get some clothing for her. When I came back to the shack the woman was gone.

By now I tried to link the many clues. The long speeches, redundantly and repeatedly given by the communist leaders, made little sense. The warning signs given by the young man, the old fellow, and the gray haired lady made much more logical sense. Why else had the communists tried so conscientiously to emphasize our safety? Why had they not given us enough food? Where were the trucks to transport us to the city? What was up with the armed guards who were patrolling and watching us like we were criminals?

The clear answer came in that late rainy afternoon, right after the sunset. Finally, the soldiers rounded us up to form a long queue waiting to be transported out. Not by truck, but by the heavy metal Chinese made bicycles. They had called us in, five to six people at a time, to be bought out through the back of the temple toward the mountains.

The Whispering Voice

"You must take the chance now because, if you don't, your dream will be over;" I thought I heard someone's voice whispering behind my ears.

I looked around. People were still waiting for their names to be called. Some children were crying. Their mothers were poking the ground nervously with small wood sticks. My heart was racing; my legs were restless and ready to move. My face seemed to get really hot as my fear was replaced by an extremely daring thought and idea. I saw a dozen soldiers pacing around several monks' houses several hundred feet away. I knew they would spray the bullets from their machine guns at me, yet I believed that I would survive. I bit my lips tightly, and a few seconds later, I felt as if someone kicked me from behind.

I jumped over the heads of the would be victims who were waiting near me, and dashed across the open ground. Suddenly, I heard deafening rounds of gunshots, and bullets were flying around me and over my head as I was spinning my feet. I thought the bullets were slower than my feet, which were dancing around them and moving as fast as they could go towards the woods. I knew that I would survive, and felt confident that my life would be saved.

I kept on running in the jungle throughout that night, using the stars as my guide, until I became too exhausted to move on any further. I finally collapsed, just a few moments after feeling that everything around me had died.

The next morning came and, as I rose from death I was saved by a young couple with a baby boy. We became brothers. The Khmer Rouge had targeted the father to be executed for being an intellectual.

Mastermind Alliance

The three of us faced the same threat—death by bloodstained hoes. We planned our escape to freedom, the freedom I saw in my mind's eye. I did not know where or what freedom really was, but I determined to get there. Patrick, the husband, and I had drawn up plans to get to Thailand.

Our mastermind alliance grew as we met Patrick's in-laws, who also wanted to escape. We met them a few days later on Route 6. We had been successful in eluding the Khmer Rouge soldiers for several nights until the soldiers in the Middle of Cambodia finally caught us. They placed us in a few houses and their pineapple eyes—soldiers and civilian agents who lived in the village, watched us closely.

Positive Mental Attitude

The Khmer Rouge authorities forced us to do heavy manual labor every single day. I knew that they were watching me and investigating me. Many people went missing every night because they had been sent to concentration (death) camps. I knew I might be next. One day I decided to change my attitude, and became cheerful at the work site instead of being grumpy, like most people were. I started to sing their revolutionary songs, and I began to love whatever I was told to do, including digging dirt to build dams. A young cadre—a pretty young girl—had noticed such my unusual attitude and reassigned me to work at a separate site as a scarecrow chasing birds from the rice field.

The Obstacles

I won the girl's heart by singing love songs, as she requested—actions that could result in death if they were reported. I had sung for her not knowing if she would send me to be killed. She gave me clues about how to get to freedom, but there were so many obstacles. The jungles were too dense. There would be no food and no water, and many people believed that I would be eaten by wild animals, killed by land mines, starve to death, shot by the Khmer Rouge, drown in the rivers, fall into the valleys or from the mountain tops and, even if I got to Thailand, Thai soldiers would gun me down. Escaping with Patrick's wife and baby with us seemed impossible.

PERSISTENCE

We had attempted to escape a few times but failed. Finally, we managed to escape the village around midnight. Only 12 of us, from different villages, managed to escape. To avoid being captured, we trekked through the woods by night and hid during the days. The little baby boy kept on crying which made the escape more dangerous.

When we got to somewhere in the middle of the woods, the soldiers captured us, and sent us to be executed. It was the second time facing execution for me.

What I have shared with you is only the beginning journey of my survival story about the pursuit of freedom. May you receive many lessons from my chapter but the one I hope that you will believe is that anything is possible if we believe in ourselves to accomplish what may seem impossible. Although, i had to reminisce many painful memories to put them in writing I am forever grateful to be able to share my story with you.

BIO

Tim Chhim was born and raised in Cambodia. At the end of the Vietnam War Tim was slated to be transported to a remote area to be killed. Tim lives in Nanuet, New York. He is an award winning Allstate agent.

Tim's dreams for freedom of body, mind and spirit began when Cambodia plunged into a war-torn country in 1970's. He visualized that he would one day come to live in the freest country on earth—the USA, even though he did not know where America was. In April 1975, when Khmer Rouge won the war against the US backed government, they began to execute millions of Cambodian freedom lovers like Tim.

Tim was one of those millions who were sent to be executed. With the picture of freedom and America in his mind Tim dreamed on. While he was waiting in a long line to be killed, along with many others, Tim jumped out of the row and ran into the nearby jungle and his journey began. Tim spent many weeks in the jungle escaping communist soldiers, wild animals, and countless landmines. He swam across rivers and climbed up numerous mountains in order to reach Thailand in August 1975.

Achieve Togetherness with Your Family

By Jeremy Rayzor

BELIEVE IN WHAT truly makes you happy, then live for what you want to achieve.

Your family should be each other's most precious possession. Each member contributes to the family's social environment, and by learning, applying, and reviewing time-tested success principles together, your family's foundation will grow stronger. Families that don't apply and review success principles can turn into a demolition team, unaware of the destruction caused by their words and actions, and not realizing how that damage affects the rest of the family. Applying time-tested success principles as a group will help to build a support team that can propel each member toward individual achievement.

I am a passionate game inventor who believes in the importance of playing board and card games as a family and, in turn, educating through the value of play. I have been creating games since I was about eight years old, although at that stage of inventing my parents reminded me that only my twin brother Jason and I knew how to play those games. One night at my childhood home in East Chicago, Indiana in 2000, which was our senior year of high school, Jason and I were playing with a regular deck of playing cards. At that moment I decided we should create our own card game, which turned out to be something we called *Switch-Up*. We had a lot of fun playing Switch-Up with our friends and family. I soon realized that I really enjoyed inventing games that provided fun entertainment designed to bring people together. After that day I knew I had discovered my passion in life. I had a burning desire to share my talent with the world by inventing more games. The support of my amazing parents, Dellard and Ada Rayzor, made it possible for me to follow my life's purpose. They have encouraged and helped me from the beginning, and their tremendous support has been the greatest gift.

Our life is what we make it. We become what we surround our mind with, which influences our future. It's made up of the music we listen to, the people we associate with, the occupation we choose, the self-development books we study, and the activities we engage in during our spare time. I made the important decision to study Napoleon Hill's philosophy because I felt the passion that he put into writing his self- development books. Napoleon Hill devoted his life to composing a practical success philosophy for the betterment of humanity. He tells us that we are in control of our own lives through the thoughts we emotionalize. We make our own decisions that will sculpt our life's journey.

THE DAY I PURCHASED THINK AND GROW RICH

I was still living in East Chicago when I graduated from college in 2004. At that time, I made the simple but powerful decision to summon up the courage and follow a friend's sincere suggestion to "Take Action Now!" and read *"Think and Grow Rich"* by Napoleon Hill. I was searching for motivation and guidance at that point in my life but after purchasing the book, I only read the introduction and laid it back down because I wasn't an avid reader at that time. I just wasn't ready for it. It wasn't until four years later in 2008 that I developed the burning desire to read *"Think and Grow Rich"*.

Before revisiting the book, I worked for two years as a substitute teacher for the School City of East Chicago and the School City of Whiting. Then I decided to move to Bozeman, Montana in late 2006. This big move was encouraged by my brother Jason who was employed, at that time, as a traveling surgical technician in Bozeman. Within three months, in the beginning of 2007, we launched a family business— Rayzor Sharp Cellular Accessories. After its first year, I was suddenly inspired to revisit my *"Think and Grow Rich"* book. This time the circumstances were different ... I was ready for it! Since then, my life's perspective has become more defined and success-oriented after taking the *Personal Initiative* to read and listen to the numerous books and audio programs provided by *The Napoleon Hill Foundation* and *Napoleon Hill World Learning Center.* I made a firm decision to learn, apply and review Napoleon Hill's time-tested philosophy throughout my life. Later, in 2012, I decided to become a *Napoleon Hill Foundation Certified Instructor* to help inspire the next generation in embracing Napoleon Hill's philosophy through the value of play. As a passionate educational board and card game inventor, I believe in fun, quality, and face-to-face human interaction. With the wisdom I have gained through Napoleon Hill's Success Philosophy, I know I will continue to create new educational games.

My parents and I founded our first family business, *Rayzor Sharp Entertainment,* in 2005, which has produced two self-development games, among our other games. Our first self-development game was created in 2011 and we named it *"Achievus"*. It's a cooperative board game combining positive interaction with Napoleon Hill's 17 principles of success using a fun-filled approach. Our second self-development game was produced in 2013, which we named *"Ticket to Wealth"* 100% Pure Mental Gold. This Napoleon Hill Leadership card game provides 100 multiple-choice challenges to learn, review, and apply the knowledge necessary to find happiness and prosperity.

Rayzor Sharp Entertainment hosts after-school and summer library programs in our local community, which uses our educational games to provide an enriching environment for families. The inspiration for inventing *"Ticket to Wealth"* came from my work with Judy Williamson, *Executive Director of the Napoleon Hill World Learning Center.* She has been a great supporter of my passion and purpose, *"Educating through the value of play"*. I am grateful for her support and honored to have worked with her to develop this new inspirational tool.

It All Starts from One's Belief in an Idea

"Whatever the mind of man can conceive and believe it
can achieve."

— Napoleon Hill

When I successfully read *"Think and Grow Rich"*, I was motivated by Napoleon Hill's and Andrew Carnegie's belief that people of the world need to learn and apply a *Magic Formula* for success. Andrew Carnegie believed Napoleon Hill's success formula should be placed within reach of people who do not have time to research how individuals achieve success and happiness in their lifetime. As I was reading, I felt an inspiration for action when I realized that this remarkable philosophy should be introduced to individuals at a young age. Being an avid game inventor, I naturally was encouraged to develop a board game that would introduce this philosophy of positive success to children as well as adults in a fun and engaging way. I didn't know how such a game would be played or how it would look but I knew I was going to do it. I was very excited and immediately began developing this concept, working on it for a long time before it was complete.

In 2010, during the development stage of my new game concept, I contacted Don M. Green, Executive Director of The Napoleon Hill Foundation. I contacted Don because I had some questions about a product I purchased from the Foundation called *"My Shadow Ran Fast"* by Bill Sands. After our conversation, he said he would send me a reprint of *"Napoleon Hill's Magazine"* as a gift. As I opened up the package, I noticed the magazine wasn't there. Instead, I had received a package intended for someone else. It was another book that I hadn't read yet titled *"Napoleon Hill's Keys to Success"* The 17 Principles of Personal Achievement. This book inspired me to incorporate Napoleon Hill's 17 Principles of Success with my game concept, soon to be called *"Achievus"*.

My family decided to take out a loan to finance the first production of Achievus, and today Achievus is supported by a growing group of more than 160 Achievus Trainers around the world. They bring the strength to the Achievus World Alliance sharing their diverse experiences, education, talents, and influence to carry out this mission. This was made possible with the direction of my friends and business partners, Takeshi Umemura (since 2011) from Japan and Aristoteles Nielson (since 2012) from Argentina. I believe Napoleon Hill would be delighted about our mission for inspiring an Achievus World together one family, business, and country at a time.

The Purpose of Achievus

Achievus coins the meaning of achieving together: achieve+us. With the combination of Napoleon Hill's philosophy "*The 17 Principles of Success*" and the game play of "*Achievus*", families now have the opportunity to learn, apply, and review this time-tested philosophy together in a fun setting. Playing Achievus instils the success principles through repetition and communication of the philosophy. While playing, players are working together to achieve a common goal. It reinforces the premise that the most important individuals closest to you need to also understand the importance of success principles if you want to be positively supported and influenced by them. Playing "*Achievus*" with your family will provide you with a quality family communication tool. We have made it a habit to play Achievus together as a family on Sundays.

While playing "*Achievus*" with younger players, the initial focus is to just have fun and spend time together. During the game, you can wait for them to ask what a principle means (which is the best time to talk with them about it because they will be curious) or periodically select a principle card and ask them what the principle means to them. If they don't know the meaning of the principle, they will naturally read the meaning on the card to provide an answer or they may ask you what it means. Either way it will encourage you and your family to discuss these important success principles in a fun and engaging way. What children learn in their pre-teen years stays with them more strongly throughout their lives. Introducing them to success principles at that age in an entertaining way will help build a positive foundation.

I often wondered what Napoleon Hill would think about the idea of introducing his 17 Principles of Success to children and adults through such a game like Achievus. Two years after producing Achievus I discovered a paragraph in his words written in Law of Success back in 1928 which made the hairs on the back of my neck stand up, he wrote… "We spend millions of dollars annually for toys to entertain our children. Make your toy useful as well as interesting. Make it educational if possible. If it entertains and teaches at the same time it will sell readily and live forever. If your toy is a game, make it teach the child something about the world, such as geography, arithmetic, English, science, and so on." I felt that Napoleon Hill should have said, "If your toy is a game, make the game teach the child something about the world, such as this success philosophy…" After thinking about this for a while I realized that it was up to me to discover this on my own to make it a reality through my own personal initiative.

With our generation's busy schedules and the impact of technology around us, it is easy to get lost in it all. We need to learn to balance everything in our lives. Setting time aside to spend with your family is very important for maintaining good communication. Playing tabletop games as a family creates a bond of common interest and encourages face-to-face communication. While playing *"Achievus"*, players will enjoy teamwork, laughter, excitement, and meaningful discussions, which are some of the most important factors behind the game.

You are the sum total of your environmental influences, including yourself. The principle strength in the roots of a family tree will determine the level of success it will grow to experience. Are you instilling time-tested success principles that build a strong foundation for your family?

Bio

JEREMY RAYZOR *is a Napoleon Hill Foundation Certified Instructor. He has been recognized as a VIP member of The Cambridge Who's Who Registry of Executives, Professionals and Entrepreneurs. Mr. Rayzor is a passionate inventor of unique card and board games that educate through the value of play. He believes in family entertainment that encourages face to face communication. He is the inventor of "PrisMix" a card game which players mix and match 12 prismatic colors to score points with prisms, "Math Wiz" a puzzle card game which encourages practicing mental arithmetic in a fun approach, "Paper Football Card Game" which players use strategic thinking and math skills, "Achievus" a cooperative board game of positive interaction which offers a fun way to learn and review Napoleon Hill's 17 Principles of Success, and "Ticket to Wealth" 100% Pure Mental Gold... a Napoleon Hill Leadership Card Game that provides 100 challenges to learn, review, and apply the knowledge necessary to earn the wealth of happiness and prosperity. Mr. Rayzor is the Co-founder of Rayzor Sharp Entertainment, Inc. The mission of his business is "Educating through the value of play!" under the slogan, "Don't Be DULL! Be Rayzor Sharp!"*

You may connect with Mr. Rayzor on LinkedIn and Facebook by first introducing yourself by sending him an email to jrrayzor@rayzorsharpent.com. Visit his company's website at www.RayzorSharpEnt.com.

LEARNING TEAMWORK THROUGH PLAY

By Vayu Yamada

AFTER BECOMING FAMILIAR with Napoleon Hill's 17 Principles of Success by playing Achievus the cooperative board game, many great things have happened to me. I gained the confidence to become an Achievus trainer, so that I could share the benefits of playing Achievus with others in Japan.

I am motivated by the golden rule, "do unto others as I want to be done to me" and have specifically learned a lot about "teamwork" by playing playing Achievus. It has been my experience that when people first play Achievus, some of them are able to quickly notice how to help others in the game. Many people do not notice the key rule for achieving the goal of the game, which is "helping each other". Some people only think about how they can achieve for themselves and do not seem to understand the meaning of "Give and Take" or "Play to help others to achieve together".

In the beginning stages of playing Achievus, I sometimes felt a little frustrated with the people who did not understand the goal of the game, even when I showed them by example again and again. This helped me gradually learn the true meaning of "Achieve Us". Now I am able to accept all the members as they are, because I am able to think about how "we" can achieve together as a team.

This experience has also changed my own personal style at work. For years I have held an event with some co-workers on an annual basis. One of the co-workers was a very slow worker, so the other employees, including myself, were frustrated about her time-consuming pace. I was always thinking that "I do a lot of work, but she does only a little."

After experiencing Achievus by playing, teaching, and applying the principles in my life I noticed that I was dividing "her" from "me" in which there was no feeling of "us". When I noticed that, I was able to accept her as she is and see her good points. From my heart I started to think of her and me as "us". I realized that even though she was slow at doing some of the work, she was an essential member when it came to bringing communication to all of the members. Eventually, the communication between members became better, and we were able to achieve the event smoothly. This is only one example among a lot of other experiences that I have learned from applying Napoleon Hill's 17 success principles.

HELPING PEOPLE BY PLAYING ACHIEVUS

While I was staying at a friend's house last year, I held Achievus workshops for two days, with eight people each day. During those two days, I had two very impressive experiences. My friend's husband is in his sixties. Two years ago, he failed in business and was in debt, so he had lost his self-confidence. The relationship between him and his wife was also not so good because of their debts, and they were speaking to each other less and less. When he first played Achievus, he quickly noticed how to achieve the goal of helping each other. He showed leadership and inspired the team. He was so excited and lively. When his wife saw this change in him it inspired her to reminisce about her school days. They were schoolmates in high school, and she told me with a smile that she still remembered his good points and what she loved about him so much. In the second game, both he and his wife played together. He always tried to help his wife and gave her the principle cards she needed to collect in the game, but she didn't notice his thoughtfulness. Her focus was always on how to help the other people. After the game, he told her that he was trying to help her. Because of playing Achievus together it brought out an important understanding about their relationship. She had realized for the first time that the same things were probably happening in their daily life. Her husband is a man of few words, so she had not noticed that he had been helping her in his own way. The next day, when they played together again, she happily received her husband's caring cards, and accepted the "Give and Take" with love, experiencing the feeling of "Achieve Us".

At the time, the husband was working at his friend's company on a temporarily basis, and on the next day after experiencing Achievus, he was scheduled to have a job interview for a possible position as a full time employee. He told me later that, before playing Achievus, he didn't have much confidence in his work because he lacked experience for the position. Then he told me that, after experiencing Achievus, he was able to regain his self-confidence again by playing the game. He said that before the interview, he kept on repeating "Applied Faith, Applied Faith" and "I believe I can!!" So when interviewers asked him "Do you really think you can do this job?" he was able to answer with confidence, "Yes, I can." When he came back home, he told us with a smile, that he was now fully employed. After that day he was able to show his leadership in the family once more. He and his wife also began talking to each other with love all over again. Soon after that, his wife was inspired to become an Achievus trainer.

THE BOY WHO MADE A DECISION

There was a boy who played Achievus with his mother. He was twelve years old at the time. He was a little shy, so I asked him "are you going to play with your mother or are you going to play on your own?" and he answered that he wanted to play on his own. He was able to understand the key points of Achievus quickly, so he helped other people by giving them principle cards that they needed to collect. After playing the game, an adult shared with the boy, "Thank you for helping me. I never imagined I would be helped the way you helped me. I am very moved by your actions." A few days later, his mother shared with me about what happened on the way home that day. He told his mother with a smile, "I helped other people today, didn't I? I want to play Achievus with my friends, and I think that all of the students at my school should play this game!!" His mother was surprised when she heard this because he was having a very hard time going to school. There were many days that he stayed home because he was school-phobic. After arriving home that day, he sat at his desk and started to study. His mother heard him repeating something in his room. She had to listen carefully to his words to understand what he was saying. To her amazement, he was saying to himself "Applied Faith, Applied Faith, I believe I can!" He had made this powerful decision on his own to repeat this positive affirmation to himself!

The next day was the annual sports day for his school. He willingly went to school with confidence. His mother and teachers were very surprised how much he had changed since the last time they saw him. They said he looked very lively and happy. I was very moved when his mother told me about this wonderful story. I never thought before that such wonderful things could actually happen by just playing a game with someone.... but they can and they did! He only played one game of Achievus and yet it had such a dramatic influence on him. When I became an Achievus trainer, I did not imagine that such things would happen. Now I feel there are endless possibilities through Achievus, because through playing the game, we can "experience" the 17 principles, and every time we play we are able to learn something new.

Bio

VAYU YAMADA has worked as a secretary for 13 years and worked as an editor for a spiritual magazine for 10 years. She has learned various kinds of therapy, art, bodywork, and meditation throughout her life. After acquiring these skills she developed a strong desire to help people to live the life they desire. This inspired her to also become a life coach, therapist and a Japanese Yoga teacher. Her work is focused on encouraging others to accept themselves as they are, with confidence. She believes by applying Napoleon Hill's 17 Principles of Success we can gain the confidence to live our dreams. As an Achievus Trainer, Vayu Yamada likes sharing Achievus with the 17 principles because through playing Achievus with joy... we can improve the world!!

My God given desire to live: from surviving to wealthy living

By Ruth Neslo

WHY DO I really badly want to live? Why can I not be, literally, beaten down in life? Why do I exist? Why, why, why?

STRONG WILL TO BE IN A BETTER PLACE.

I was born in Surinam, a country North of Brazil formerly colonized by the Netherlands, in Paramaribo city 47 years ago. My parents were not married and my father left my mother during the pregnancy. After I was born, my father denied that I was his child and even brought my mother to court to deny I was his child. Back then there were no DNA tests, but because I looked Chinese and my dad is half Chinese, the judge could see clearly that I was his daughter. Despite the ruling, my father never did anything for me. During my first year I was deadly sick, was hospitalized, did not get better, and I did not want to stay there. My mother signed me out of the hospital, and had to sign a paper, which declared that if something would happen to me or I would die that she would be responsible.

As soon as I left the hospital, I got better. My mother was a single mom and I was the seventh child. She then fell in love with my stepfather, got pregnant again, and left all her children behind with different families and immigrated to the Netherlands. I was left with a family who came from India, a Hindu family. When that happened, I got sick again and would not eat anymore because I missed my mother so much. Because of that episode, I developed hair loss and my growth was stunted. One day my aunt on my mother's side passed by and she saw me in the garden of the house. I was 2 ½ years old at the time. She immediately took me out of there and sent my mother a letter. She wrote that all the other kids were doing fine in the other families but I was the only one who refused to eat and was resisting the situation. She wrote to my mother that she had to come and get me otherwise I would die.

My picture from my first passport is one where I have almost no hair and am looking very sad. I still have it to remind me where I came from.

MY DEFINITE MAJOR PURPOSE WAS SURELY TO DO BETTER, TO SURVIVE, TO PROTEST A SITUATION I DID NOT LIKE.

It's not where you are coming from but where you are going.

When I got to Holland my baby brother was already born, and I was really jealous of him. I could not speak very well but my non-verbal behavior was obvious clear. My first clothes were for a baby instead of small child because my growth had been stunted so much.

My stepfather had been physically abusing my mother for 17 years, and during those years he physically abused me as well. The first time it happened, I was 6 years old and he beat me with his boots, which caused me to wet my pants. A lot happened in my family which was just not right. At the age of 15 I got beaten up so badly that my teeth were seriously injured. My stepfather beat me with by kneeing me in the mouth. It was past midnight and I ran to my nephew, who lived around the corner, and he brought me to the hospital. I received more then twenty injections in my mouth before they got my teeth straight with an iron bracket. There was blood all over me. That day I decided to leave home and live my own life.

At school I was somebody. I received A's throughout elementary school and the teachers liked my cleverness and thought I knew a lot for my young age. I attended a Catholic school and liked all the Bible stories especially, David and Goliath. I liked to read and was always eager to learn. School was the only place I could be myself. Outside I liked to play boys stuff like soccer and climbing trees and I was very streetwise. These things helped me forget about home. I was in a "black" elementary school and, because of my good grades; I was allowed to attend a "white" high school. This changed my life for good.

There was another world, which I was totally unaware of. Another culture, other families, other people. I learned a lot, and realized that it was possible to have a good life. This helped me to have faith and believe that I could have a better future than my past.

DETERMINATION AND APPLIED FAITH EVEN THOUGH YOU HAVE TO LEAVE BEHIND THE PEOPLE YOU LOVE.

Things got bad at school because of the trauma I experienced from my physical abuse. I became demotivated, and experienced a lot of grief over my mother and leaving her and my brothers behind with my stepfather.

I got pregnant when I was seventeen years old and I knew this was not what I planned to start my better future.

I wanted to be an entrepreneur and to have my own store when I was growing up. I always liked to sell and be creative with ways to earn money. This desire was developed because I had to take care of the family when I was 8, taking care of my youngest brother, steering the household and doing groceries at the market.

ADVERSITY AND DEFEAT CARIES WITHIN THE SEED OF SUCCESS IF YOU LOOK FOR IT.

My pregnancy reminded me of my first definite major purpose which was to have a better life. I got motivated because I had sworn in my youth that my future children would never have the life and especially the childhood, which I had. This was my commitment.

I left home, because of the bad situation, when I was fifteen and decided to get the best out of life. I believed that there must be something better out there for me. With that belief, and my commitment to my son to give him a better life, I had to discipline myself. I had to control my emotions. I had to structure my life. I had to plan, and be very careful with my time.

So I went back to school and studied. While I was raising my son, I studied and worked at the same time. I have also raised two daughters and have my own business. I play sports and also have leisure time. I could not do all this without a huge dose of self-discipline. While others were partying, I read books. While others had someone they could share finances with, I only had my income to rely on. While others had their company or parents pay for their education, I paid all mine by myself and still do today.

Today, my son helps me with my second business; my eldest daughter has 5 businesses and maintains the top spot in her martial arts. My youngest daughter practices gymnastics more than twelve hours a week and won third place at the Dutch National Championship. Children do not listen to what you say but they do model what you do.

Also I respect and love my parents and forgave them for all what has happened to free myself.

There is no achievement without Self-Discipline and therefore no progress in your definite major purpose. Discipline yourself, and the channel through which all personal power of success must flow will be unleashed.

Definiteness of purpose is the starting point of all achievement. To achieve you need Self-Discipline, which is the process that ties all your efforts together. Efforts like taking control of your mind, a positive mental attitude, personal initiative and others. Self- Discipline requires Self-knowledge - know thyself. To know yourself takes time, and a conscious choice to invest in your personal development. This is how you create personal power.

With my willpower, combined with the desire to have a better life for children,
and myself and my dream of being a successful entrepreneur I have achieved
a lot of my goals.

Bio

For over 14 years Ruth Neslo has fulfilled interim functions. She started her com-
pany Busy-Nes in 1997. In addition

She also has 25 years of experience in finance and has had over 65 compa-
nies as clients. She has helped finance departments with financial services and
guided them through transition phases after reorganizations. She moved up from
bookkeeping assistant to become Manager of Business Operations, HR Manager,
Finance Controller.

Ruth has served several company branches, multinational corporations,
SME's and start-ups. She is an energetic achiever who has invested a lot of time,
money and focus into personal effectiveness and communication. This has helped
her to develop her leadership skills and which adds great value for companies and
departments, especially those in crisis. She creates stability and is solution and
goal oriented in her work.

Ruth is very operational and has managerial abilities: "The person behind the
figures" is her motto!

Ruth has spent a lot of time and money on training, courses and seminars
and has read a lot of books on business economics and personal and organiza-
tional development.

She has combined motherhood, business, studying, personal development, fi-
nance, entrepreneurship, real estate and taking care of her own finances for more
than 30 years. This was not without experiencing adversity and defeats, which
she overcame.

The strong development of her energy, power, communication, passion and
perseverance, and creating the life that fits her is what Ruth wants to share to
motivate and inspire others.

The development of her personality has been reinforced with a number of methodologies including; Neuro Logistic Programming (NLP), Napoleon Hill principles and systemic work breaking negative family patterns.

Her passion is to support people and organizations to STRENGTHENING THEMSELVES by transforming their communication using tools they already have, or can develop. She is convinced that everyone can increase and improve their abilities and talents by communicating to yourself and others in a powerful way.

She is a grateful and happy woman and wants to contribute and share to make this world a better place.

At this moment she is Manager Finance and Accounting at the finance department of Nippon Seiki in the Netherlands and is guiding them through their transition phase.

Ruth is launching the "Neslo Institute" with the goal of transforming your communication and results through training, coaching, workshops, and motivational speaking.

Ruth is the only Dutch/Surinamees woman to be certified as a Napoleon Hill Foundation Instructor and is also an International Certified NLP trainer and motivational speaker.

Ruth's websites are:
www.ruthneslo.com
www.nlpnetherlands.com for NLP information
www.richmind.nl for Napoleon Hill information

Using PMA to Live Positively With Chronic and Never-Ending Pain

By Tom "Too Tall" Cunningham

Maintaining a Positive Mental Attitude when you live in constant and never-ending pain is extremely difficult. It takes constant awareness of your thoughts, and deliberate refocusing of them and it must be practiced consistently.

You never get used to living in constant and never-ending pain throughout your body. You never get halfway through your day and think to yourself, "I didn't realize I was sore today". Even if you have a very positive mental attitude, the constant awareness of pain can cause your thoughts, words, and cautions to be negative and harmful.

Since I was diagnosed with Rheumatoid Arthritis (RA) throughout my body at the age of 5, I cannot remember ever not being in pain. I am 52 years old at the time of this writing in the 47 years since my initial diagnosis; I have had 4 hips, 4 knees and 2 shoulders replaced.

I also had cataracts removed at the age of 12 due to the high daily dose of prednisone I was forced to take to fight the disease. Around the age of 25, I had intraocular lens implants, where they surgically insert something like a contact lens behind your eye. You are also awake for the surgery, which adds some stress before the surgery when thinking about it.

The worst surgery I ever survived was a right ankle fusion when I was about 27 years old. Doctors had to break bones and reshape them so my foot would be fused at a functional 90 degree angle rather than fusing haphazardly at an awkward angle. The recovery from that surgery was long and difficult, much more than any surgery I have ever had. I was forced to move in with my sister and her husband so they could help me with day to day living. I was not able to put weight on the foot for 6 weeks, which, considering my left leg was not in good shape to take all that extra work, made it extra difficult. It was also during this period that I had to go without a car and driving for 4 months. I had owned and car since I was 16 and the thought of having to take a handicapped bus everywhere I went was depressing for me.

Most of my joints are either completely fused and do not bend at all or they have a very low range of motion. Along with the aches and pains, the mobility challenges I have to overcome make life tough at the best of times.

It is impossible to endure that much pain and so many surgeries and hospital visits without suffering from periods of depression. Just recently, I went through a 3 week period where I kept thinking about how I would feel and how mobile I would be in 20 years, when I am in my 70's. Since I feel like I am 80 years old every day now, how will it feel then? Those thoughts occupied my thinking and my focus and, unlike what usually happens automatically, I did not refocus those thoughts back to the MANY positives and blessings in my life. When you speak from the stage about why it is important to do that and then you don't do it yourself, it feels hypocritical, which made the negative thinking cycle worse of course.

From this episode, and others I have endured throughout 47 years of not having a single second without pain in 3 or more joints and achiness throughout my body, I have learned a few things that I hope and pray will help you to live positively through your challenges and help you regain your positivity when your thoughts get you down.

PURPOSEFULLY AND CAREFULLY CHOOSE YOUR THOUGHTS

Napoleon Hill's book Think and Grow Rich starts with the words "Thoughts are things". I was around 22 years old when I took a Raymond Aaron real estate investing course. Part of the course was a suggested list of books to read. While at one of the meetings, I met Shane Morand,

Co-Founder of Organo Gold, the official Partner of The Napoleon Hill Foundation. Shane flat out told me to read Think and Grow Rich first after a very enthusiastic sales presentation on the value of the book.

After reading that book, I learned, and have practiced for many years now, purposefully choosing my thoughts. We all have about 60,000 thoughts daily, and if we do not take charge of our thoughts and monitor them constantly, the negative news networks of the world will fill your thinking with thoughts of anger, sadness, and despair and every possible negative thoughts and emotions you can imagine.

One way to purposefully choose your thoughts is to come up with several affirmations that you can repeat to yourself whenever your mind slips to the dark side and you are dwelling on things that upset you. By constantly monitoring your thoughts, you get quicker at interrupting your bad thoughts and replacing them with affirmations that you have pre-chosen. Along with those affirmations, have a mental movie that you play in your mind that helps you reinforce your God given life purpose and visualize what you will be doing and how you will be living.

If you are married, you know about having negative thoughts, and perhaps dwelling on those thoughts, from time to time. I can see you nodding your head on that one. Guess what? I do the same thing. Because of the 30 years of training my thoughts, I am able to quickly recognize when this is happening and I am able to redirect that thinking to the many good times we have had, and some affirmations and visualization of our future. I live in Toronto, which experiences cold and tough winters. One of my affirmations is "We spend the winter months in a warm climate". I have a visualization of that as well. The practice of constantly monitoring my thoughts helps me to redirect those thoughts and emotions very quickly.

GET AND STAY BUSY

Not only have I experienced periods of depression, I have also led depression support groups at church. Almost everyone who gets depressed starts to withdraw from life in various ways.

During my most recent 3 weeks of depression, I barely read any non-fiction books. Since I regularly read 40-50 non-fiction books yearly so, barely reading for 3 weeks is totally out of character.

I also stopped going to the gym for a month. I gave in to the same excuses I have ignored for the 14 years I have been working out. I am ALWAYS tired and sore and so I have a built-in excuse. I have worked out 3-4 times weekly for long enough that I know to ignore those excuses. During my 3 week episode, I gave in to the excuses and stayed home.

My wife Kim and I almost always have a hectic social calendar, and I am the one who arranges most of it. I have many amazing friends and like to meet in person to catch up. During my 3 weeks of depression, our social calendar was pretty quiet and I did not spend much face to face time with my closest and dearest friends.

You will absolutely have to force yourself during times when you are depressed, or thinking negatively, to do what you know you should do, and have said you will do. At those times, if at all possible, get active and stay active. True happiness and joy comes from being around people. Studies and interviews with the elderly overwhelmingly tell us that the time they spent with people they loved was the source of almost all their happiness and joy. Their possessions are forgotten, or not mentioned.

I urge you to get actively involved in the outside world in various ways. To truly live positively, you need to help people who you can help, and learn from people who can help you use more of your God given skills, talents, and abilities.

JOIN A WEEKLY MASTERMIND GROUP

Of Napoleon Hill's 17 Principles of Success, the Mastermind Alliance was the only one he claimed to have come up with as an original principle, and maybe even word or phrase. Hill got the idea directly from Andrew Carnegie, because one of Carnegie's greatest strengths was hiring the best people on the planet for their specific jobs and those people became his inner mastermind group.

I am in an amazing mastermind group www.compassmastermind.com with Napoleon Hill Foundation Instructors from around the world. We keep each other accountable to our purposes and goals. We encourage and support each other. Each member of the group also goes out of the way to help each other.

The benefits of meeting weekly with like minded people, who all help each other pursue their life's purpose and goals is one of the surest ways to make the most of your time, skills, talents and abilities.

Two things of vital importance you must have when starting and continuing a mastermind group are; 1) The right people in the group and 2) perfect harmony within the group. Invite people to your mastermind group who will make you a better person, because becoming a better you will be the main thing that will help you achieve your purpose and goals. Don't just choose people you know and like. Keep them as friends but do not have them in your mastermind group, unless they truly bring out the very best in you and are also pursuing their own goals and life purpose.

When you go through tough times, and periods of depression and negativity, your mastermind members will encourage you, and help you to get through the tough times while remaining focused on your life's purpose and goals.

Life is tough! You need a chosen group of people, who you meet with weekly, either in person or online, using tools like Skype and Google Hangout, that you can open your thoughts and feelings to without reservation.

I have experienced the deeply intimate and encouraging experience of mastermind groups and have found them to be a great source of encouragement and inspiration. Having those people in your corner and on your calendar every week will become invaluable to you.

Bio

Tom (too tall) Cunningham is a Napoleon Hill Foundation Certified Instructor and Resiliency Expert. He is the Founder and a Host of

Journey To Success Radio. Tom has shared the stage with Deepak Chopra, Jim Rohn, Mark Victor Hansen, Frank Shankwitz (Founder of the Make A Wish Foundation), Dave Liniger (Co-Founder with his wife of Re/Max Real Estate) and Jeffrey Gitomer. His list of interviewees for his radio show is just as impressive.

Tom was diagnosed with Juvenile Rheumatoid Arthritis at the age of 5. It affects every joint in his body from his jaw to his toes. He has had 4 knees, 4 hips, and 2 shoulders replaced and been hospitalized about 40 times.. Most of his joints have very limited range of motion, or are totally fused.

Despite his physical challenges, Tom always answers AMAZING when asked how he is doing. He tells people that 80% of the time it is true and the other 20% of the time it is to remind himself that it is true.

Find out more about Tom at www.tom2tall.com

Life is About Choices, What do you Choose?

By Marianne Noad

Is NOW THE time to get over being weighed down by your past? What if living can be much easier and rewarding than you thought possible? I am inviting you to expand beyond the limitations you think are real. Only you can decide to begin a new journey... Here is my story of transition.

As I write these words I am listening to beautiful classical music, in a cozy log house on a peaceful secluded island off the coast of Western Canada. A short walk from this oasis the deep blue waters of the North Pacific Ocean gently greets the shoreline.

Every morning upon waking I always take time to whisper words of gratitude for this blessed life. At times I almost feel the need to pinch myself to make sure I am not dreaming... Or could it be I am living my dream?

Seven short years ago my life was much different, stark in comparison to now. In 2008 I was a single mother of 3 beautiful children, struggling financially. Stress was my companion along with long workdays.

I had a small clinic in Central Alberta. Being a holistic health practitioner brought me great satisfaction on a career level. However it seemed like there was never enough hours in the day to meet all the demands of family and work. Personal time was pretty well non-existent and I fantasized about having the luxury of time for ME. At the end of every month I agonized over which bill to pay and which one would have to wait. It felt like financial Russian roulette, would the phone be disconnected... Or the power shut off... You see I had declared personal bankruptcy years prior.

There were no credit cards, business loans or line of credit to run the business from. My ability to budget and know where every dollar went was a talent I developed. Every year with my head held high and an optimistic posture I would venture into the bank to ask for assistance. The story I heard over and over again was "sorry we can't help you." Being a woman over 40 years old, self-employed, without a husband (god forbid), I was considered too risky, no matter what my business books looked like. Even though my income increased year after year with no debt, the banks continued to deny my applications. Could it be I was a credit leper?

Life continued on and it was my priority to maintain a positive attitude and be grateful for what I did have. A happy home life, thriving kids with great friends and my own business that kept my family fed, housed and clothed. My motto was (and still is) You are not defined by what you own, but who you are as a person. Be generous with kindness, laughter and tolerance.

Quite a few of my clients knew of my circumstances and often suggested that I should look for a husband to improve my situation... That was never an option I entertained or understood. Don't get me wrong; I think marriage can be a fulfilling and sacred union between two people. You don't just snap your fingers and Mr. Right shows up.

What I did do was immerse myself in personal development books and seminars. The information was empowering and exciting, almost like a drug. I could not get enough. New concepts flooded my mind and I embraced the difference between reactive thought and proactive thought. Realizing that the belief systems given to me turned out to be a detriment to my life, I began to practice awareness. Epiphanies and pivoting moments started to bring clarity, quenching my thirst to evolve and create new outcomes in my life. Was it my imagination... Or was my life actually changing? Whispers of doubt still tried to influence me but my heightened awareness would sweep them away. Doors began to open and the right people started to show up. Often when I shared these exhilarating insights with others, many times I encountered smug smiles or blank stares. I was breaking away from mainstream belief systems. Over time I realized that it didn't matter what others thought of me. What people think of me is none of my business; it is what I think of me that matters. Breaking away from the herd mentality (this is not intended to insult anyone) came with some heartache. It was crucial for my metamorphosis, to leave or minimize my time with negative or fearful people. It was true… you become more like the people you hang out with.

Much to my delight my coaches and evolved mentors taught that spirituality and financial wealth were intertwined, a stark comparison to what I had been taught as a young girl, that money was the root of all evil. It was a belief system that I divorced, never to be reconciled. Guilt and shame had to go also, a process that is easier said than done.

Gradually pieces of the puzzle were coming together and I was experiencing life on a level of growing synchronicity. Soon I found myself surrounded with like-minded people. It was refreshing and safe to speak my truth and empowering thoughts. They spoke the same or similar language, giving me support and encouragement. It takes the same energy to dream big as it does to dream small… My dreams were massive.

Then one day it happened!! Shane Morand a friend and successful businessman called me. Shane spoke of a new business venture he was involved in. The founder of this company Mr. Bernard Chua was also someone I knew and respected (coincidence I think not). Shane shared their vision and dream for this new company; I felt a strange energy start to run through my body. Both of these men had great integrity, courage and a deep desire to make a difference in this world. They also had brilliant minds and a track record of success in business. The phone call lasted over an hour but seemed like five minutes. Time stood still and I felt a sense of excitement mixed in with relief. There was a strong intuitive knowing that this was MY opportunity to free others and myself. To make the world a better place. I have always been a purpose driven person so it was important to me that whatever I do was making a difference in people's lives. When he extended the invitation to join them in the business there was no hesitation on my part. Now remember this is February 2008 just as the global recession was hitting everyone hard... Fear and anxiety was high.

I shared this opportunity with others not really understanding all the nuts and bolts of the business model. Armed with optimism and strong belief I started down this new path. It was important to learn new skills and be coachable. In order to have something different you must become something different. I did have my moments... Being an entrepreneur and owning my own businesses for decades I had some bad habits. Accepting that I was responsible for where I was in life was a humbling experience, but also a great realization to make a change. Shane imparted wisdom and guidance along with a lot of patience. I was a sponge, soaking up this new method of doing business. My background had been traditional business and now I was learning about network marketing. I know a few of you are now allowing some negative thoughts to pop into your mind at this very moment, but bear with me. Due to the fact that this was a network marketing company, many people rolled their eyes and were very condescending. It surprised me there was so much myth, prejudice and ignorance about this industry. I had also heard many stories of people's negative experiences in network marketing, and the majority of the time I recognized that it was due to lack of training, leadership, motivation and personal development. In this company our motto was we leave no one behind, everyone deserves a chance to realize their dreams.

It was time to put my 'big girl panties' on and move forward building my dream. Fortunately for me many opened minded entrepreneurs and traditional business people recognized the massive coffee market and were impressed with the lucrative and unique compensation plan. People were waking up and smelling the coffee (and not in Brazil) here with me! Business was flowing and so was the money.

This is where the rubber hit the road for me, Shane introduced the book 'Think and Grow Rich' by Napoleon Hill to me. This book was the missing pieces of my life puzzle. I read and re-read it, putting into practice the magical 17 principles. To this day I am still working on and implementing them all into my life. It requires commitment and awareness plus action, but the rewards far outweigh the growth pains. I will expand on this later.

My energy levels were high, my spirit strong, my days long and very busy. Now I was juggling kids, full time work at my clinic, and building my Organo Gold part time coffee business.. wheew! A family meeting was called where the kids and I got together to set goals and become a team. They had to take on additional responsibilities and not see Mom hardly at all. It was decided that when we reached specific goals, we would celebrate and reward ourselves. It was the first success team I ever built. This was crucial as I really needed their cooperation and help. Within 9 hectic months I retired my full time J-O-B (clinic) and focused solely on my Organo Gold business. In life when you are building something great, sacrifices are necessary, was it worth it... Hell yeah!

Months passed and my business grew along with my income. I caught myself one day regretting that I had not been introduced to the book 'Think and Grow Rich' earlier. My remorse was centered on the time missed with my children. A mother's guilt can run deep, but that was in the past. The guilt was replaced with deep gratitude for the many gifts I had received. An inner voice urged me to focus on the present (it truly is a gift) and whose life I could have a positive impact on.

Single mothers would hear my stories and ask if this could work for them also. I would respond "If an average, struggling single mom like me could do it why couldn't they" was always my answer. It was a deep honor to work with my growing teams but the single moms always had a special place in my heart.

Life continued to improve on so many levels – personally, financially, health wise and spiritually. It was fun and rewarding to do this business and I immersed myself in it. It became a daily focus to implement the new tools I was learning into my life. The old belief that I had to work hard to create income was replaced with the lightness and fun of being paid to drink and share coffee, talk and travel the world. Meeting amazing people in places like: China, Jamaica, Australia, Mexico, USA and Canada just to name a few. It was a paradigm shift for me. In the beginning I worked hard for smaller commissions and now I was beginning to enjoy the power of exponential numbers, the business was flourishing and so was I. It was evident that I was attracting the 17th principle of 'Think and Grow Rich'... Cosmic Habitforce.

> And I quote "Cosmic Habitforce pertains to the universe as a whole and the laws that govern it. Cosmic Habitforce is infinite intelligence in operation. It is a sense of order. It takes over a habit and causes a person to act upon the habit automatically. Developing and establishing positive habits leads to peace of mind, health, and financial security. You are where you are and what you are because of your established habits, thoughts and deeds".

> – Napoleon Hill

One of the 17 principles that I had unknowingly been practicing most of my life was principle # 7, a positive mental attitude. I believe that it was what sustained me during my earlier life. In my opinion it is the first habit that people require to begin their transformation. Sometimes you must fake it before you make it. Even if you are having a crappy day you don't have to spew your problems on everyone and everything in your path. "Where thoughts go, energy flows" is a popular phrase... but it is also a fact. Going the Extra Mile principle # 4, and #12 Teamwork were key factors in my business team's growth.

Through my awareness I realized that big and small miracles were happening to me on a daily basis. In my opinion one of the biggest miracles that I witnessed was when Organo Gold and the Napoleon Hill World Learning Center created an alliance. As a company we were given the utmost privilege of this union. Many of us were excited and honored to promote the great book 'Think and Grow Rich' with our company insignia on the cover. This was a historical moment and continues to be as we were the first and only company to ever be trusted with this unique collaboration. Reading the book is the equivalent of being given a blank cheque, IF... you put it into practice.

As a company it is our responsibility to share this treasure with all of our representatives with 100% of sales proceeds given back to the Napoleon Hill World Learning Center. At this point I have lost track of how many copies of this book I have gifted to others. Knowing the importance of giving back and the joy it brings me, I decided to award 2 exceptional people annually from my business organization full tuition scholarships for the Napoleon Hill Certification course. This course expands on the 17 principles taking people to higher levels of knowledge. These are always held in exotic locations worldwide. My gift was watching the transformation of these deserving individuals, people who had exemplified leadership, positive mental attitudes, focus and belief. It was always evident throughout the year who would receive a scholarship.

Who would know that through this process one of the fringe benefits I received was connecting with the brilliant and dynamic Judith Williamson director of the Napoleon Hill World Learning Center. It was a breath of fresh air to speak with her numerous times on the phone. Not only was she inspiring but a great source of knowledge, and guidance. Last year I attended the course with 2 of my team in beautiful Victoria BC, Canada. It is an experience and a memory that I will cherish for the rest of my life.

Just when I thought life could not get any better, I received an unexpected phone call from a very close friend. (He and I went back years to when we were in our later teens. There was always a special bond between us but life turned our paths in opposite directions). We were both single and began a new long distance relationship that quickly became romantic in nature. Exactly one year and eight days later we were married at a castle by the ocean. Close friends and family witnessed our fairy tale wedding and joined us in the celebration of this old love, renewed and fulfilled finally. Glenn and I are proof that Cosmic Habitforce is indeed a force to be reckoned with. Love was right on time.

> I cannot always control what goes on outside but I can always control what goes on inside.

> –WAYNE DYER

Bio

My mission is to inspire women to rise up, seize their personal power and accept all parts of themselves. Napoleon Hill 'Think and Grow Rich' was the missing piece of my puzzle after searching for answers on my 25 year quest for enlightenment. My full journey to discovery is in my chapter of the book Napoleon Hill – Inspired Stories.

After my certification I find myself expanding into new international coffee markets. I continue to seek new people to help solve their financial pressures through the simplicity of offering someone a coffee. My newest project is developing a women's retreat center on a beautiful remote island in the Pacific Ocean. Women attending the retreat center will be introduced to the Napoleon Hill 17 Success Principles as part of the program.

Marianne Noad is a dynamic and inspiring Leader, she will believe in you until you believe in yourself. Her wisdom and knowledge in Business comes from many years of experience, including some good challenges. Inspiring others is a natural gift for Marianne, it amazing how many lives she has touched. I'm so proud to call her my mentor and my inspiration. Love you Marianne.
Rhinda Piche

Of all our experience with Marianne, what stands out the most is that her massive success in business and in every aspect of her life, is predominantly attributable to her never dwindling, positive mental attitude. It is both refreshing and tremendously motivating to work with and learn from someone with such a zest for life. She is carefree yet focused; an ambitious trailblazer but also incredibly observant. Her solid leadership comes with a compassion and sensitivity that only someone acting as a true ally in life can exhibit. Marianne's energy and light will cause personal development to rub off on you just from being in her vicinity! We cherish every valuable moment we get to spend with her. It's no coincidence that Marianne and Ganoderma found each other – they are BOTH treasures of the earth!

Mike and Jerrilynn Rebeyka

It has been my pleasure and honor to first have Marianne Noad as a close personal friend and secondly as a business partner. I have known and worked personally with Marianne for almost 10 years now. What is so special about Marianne is her willingness to always put other people first in all things. Her ability to create solutions in business with people all around the world is truly a blessing for all that have ever had a chance to work with her. Marianne has a very sharp business mind. Her dedication, persistence, and never give up attitude is truly world class. Her always-positive mental attitude is contagious as well as burning desire for other to discover their true inner champion is something I truly am grateful for.

Steve Martin

Follow or contact Marianne:
Website – www.marianne.myorganogold.com
Facebook – Marianne Noad
Email – coffeemarianne@me.com

Standing Strong on the Wings of My Dreams

By Shadiya Zackaria

"Cherish your vision and your dreams as they are the children of your soul, the blue prints of your ultimate achievements."

-Napoleon Hill

Childhood Dreams

I had two childhood dreams that I used to cherish; one of becoming a schoolteacher and the other of becoming a journalist. Two dreams, because I had two innate talents; teaching and creative writing. I have had a flair for teaching from a very early age. I used to teach commerce and accountancy to my cousins and friends in our neighborhood, while still in school.

I knew I had a special talent because these children came to me without missing classes and, their parents encouraged them as their grades improved. All these 'students' of mine came to me because they hated commerce and accountancy, and looked to me as a ray of hope in navigating through their school exam safely.

Not only did these children pass their exams with flying colors, most of them also developed a liking for these subjects and pursued their higher studies in these fields. I steered this passion forward by regularly visiting a children's orphanage located close to my home, after school, to teach the children living there. I chose this student community project as I loved serving the less fortunate. I loved teaching and helped change the direction of many students who sought my assistance with their studies.

I was equally passionate about writing and have contributed many articles and short stories to the children's section in the local newspapers and creative writing competitions held by my college. I particularly excelled in creative writing. I remember, when I wrote essays on general knowledge topics which I had no idea of, I still scored marks even though the essays were totally off the topic, only because the teacher was so carried away by my writing that she continued reading.

My most memorable moment was when I won my very first prize in school for creative writing. I still have the gold, genuine leather bonded book, "The Adventures of Huckleberry Finn" by Mark Twain, which was awarded to me as the first place prize. I believe the ability to teach and write are unique gifts that Mother Nature bestows on a person, especially on a child. But sadly, my dreams were shattered even before it could blossom. Due to pressure from home to pursue a financially rewarding career, I was compelled to accept a bank job immediately after I graduated from college. Grudgingly, and rebelliously, I started a new chapter in my life as an unwilling banker.

A Rebellious Life Takes a Surprising Twist

I continued my life as a young banker, frequently rebelling and causing distress to my parents. As years flew by, tragedy struck me in 1998 when I lost my dad. In a batter of an eyelid, a massive and sudden heart attack had cruelly snatched him away from me forever. There was no time for goodbyes, no time for apologies, no time to say "I love you dad". It was too late for that. Being the only child in the family, I was totally devastated.

My dad's demise however, stirred a strong sense of family duty in me. I decided to shoulder the responsibility of caring and providing for my family all by myself. I persuaded my mom to resign from her job. She was totally shattered by the loss of her soul mate, and I felt it was time she took a rest from her fast-paced corporate life, and stopped worrying about running our home. I gave up rebelling and took banking very seriously, focusing on career advancement, so that I could continue maintaining our standard of living. After all, I still had a passion to live for - reading! I have always been an avid reader since childhood and have read hundreds of books. I particularly enjoyed reading detective fiction and mystery books.

During the year 2010, I began developing an interest in reading self-development books, and literature on diverse universal subjects. The first book that swept me completely away from the world of fiction and into my newfound world of self-development literature was "The Seven Habits of Highly Effective People" by Stephen Covey. This book, with lessons on creating transformation from the inside out, caused a revolution in my life. But my true awakening came, when I happened to pick up a book titled **"Think & Grow Rich"** while browsing through a bookstore in 2011. This book made such a powerful impact on me that I went out in search of other books by Napoleon Hill, and was introduced to the **"Law of Success"** that came in four volumes. Reading these books caused a complete paradigm shift in the way I perceived myself, other people and life.

As a banker I had a hectic work schedule and with studies for banking exams taking up most of my spare time, I did not have enough time to indulge in my passion – reading. However, I managed to bridge this gap by reading while commuting to work daily. I used the travelling time to deeply reflect and resonate with the principles I learned. I also used commuting time to dream and envision my future. I built many magnificent castles in the air and these castles had nothing to do with banking.

The Seventeen Principles and the **Philosophy of Success** discussed by Dr. Hill resonated so well with me that I immediately started to incorporate them into my life and began to see a rapid transformation in my attitude and mindset. I especially enjoyed reflecting on, and practicing, the principle of 'Autosuggestion' or 'Self-suggestion'. Just like Dr. Hill describes in his book, I too had my own mastermind group who sat at an imaginary round table in my bedroom, where my self-development plans were drawn. My mastermind group consisted of a team of eight illustrious individuals who were internationally celebrated speakers, writers, entrepreneurs and political leaders, who had made the greatest impact on me at the time. These extraordinary achievers, had undaunted determination and courage to achieve their goals, and I naturally identified with them, and considered them as my personal mentors. Dr. Hill himself, led these meetings, and often chided me, when I fell short of expectation. I thoroughly enjoyed these imaginary meetings.

These make-believe mastermind sessions continued for approximately a year, till I had mastered the principles sufficiently enough, to proceed on my journey towards accomplishment on my own. Thereafter, I went on to read most of Dr. Hill's books, and each month I continue to add more books published by the Napoleon Hill Foundation, to my library.

Although my passion for teaching was still alive, I did not take any action to pursue this talent. In the same year, I had the good fortune of joining a Toastmasters Club in my home town. 'Toastmasters International' is a non-profit educational organization that teaches public speaking and leadership skills to its members, through a network of clubs around the world. I found a new avenue to focus my passion on. I started to specialize as a motivational speaker, selecting appropriate topics to deliver speeches at my Toastmasters club meetings. I discovered that I could inspire people, because I was a good speaker, and, above all, I spoke from my heart direct to the hearts of the audience. Joining Toastmasters motivated me to take action and get certified as a Professional Trainer, a Life Coach and a Hypnotherapist; all disciplines requiring the ability of communicating effectively and connecting instantly with people.

However, I was not given an opportunity in my bank to transfer from branch banking to training and development, nor of using any of my new skills. My request for consideration was outright rejected. And, the articles that I eagerly submitted to be published in the bank's in-house magazine were also declined. Three years down the line, practicing Dr. Hill's philosophy, experiencing the transformation it created in my life, and firmly believing in my ability to succeed, I made a resolution to leave the bank and take up training and coaching. A definite chief aim, given wings by passion, before long, gave me the courage and the confidence, to dream of launching my own training and coaching business, where many people would benefit and succeed in their lives.

A Vision of Service Sparked by Courage

My newfound confidence helped me immensely, when I started an initiative to form a Toastmasters club in my bank. Unfortunately, there were a handful of seniors who did not want to cooperate, despite there being top management approval to form the club. They made it very difficult for the staff to participate in the club meetings. But I was determined to form this club in the bank before I left, so that people would find proper direction for their lives. It was my last opportunity to give back in gratitude to my organization; in return for the financial stability and prestige it had given me.

My major purpose at the time was to form this club at any cost. And I was ready to battle it out for as long as it took. I struggled for a year to form this club because of the obstacles thrown in my way. I was penalized daily at work, and not given my due promotion and performance ratings. Sadly, during these challenging times, I was compelled to witness many repulsive facets of human nature. Nevertheless, a burning desire to succeed, staunch self-confidence, razor sharp focus and going the extra mile helped me to finally make this club a reality.

A pleasing personality helped me to win the loyalty of the first twenty prospective club members to stand by me till the club was finally formed, even though they feared their bosses and the possible repercussions of supporting me. I stood my ground in the face of all adversity, to start a Toastmasters club in my organization and, it was officially chartered in June 2014.

I am happy to say, we have a team of budding public speakers now, who have developed confidence to speak and lead. Many of them have started to win speech contests against other clubs in the area and division, which is highly commendable. All because of a vision of service sparked by courage, and the tenacity to make it a reality.

When I eventually resigned, the bank management requested me to continue assisting the club. Today, I am officially serving as district appointed club mentor. All those who worked against this noble endeavor are now part of the club, applauding and endorsing my effort. I am appreciated and remembered by all, even though I am no longer an employee, because of the Toastmasters club that I was successful in forming, standing strong against all odds. This recognition is entirely due to the personal power derived by learning and practicing Dr. Hill's teachings.

Forming this club, is an accomplishment that is sweetly gratifying to me, as, for some time now, a team of senior Toastmaster leaders, have been attempting to form a club in my organization, with little success, and I am thrilled to be the one to finally make it happen. This proves that nothing in life is impossible; all that is needed is a burning desire and willpower to succeed. My burning desire to transform the lives of my fellow work mates, have taken wings and would continue to carry forward the positive change in the bank.

A Daring Leap of Faith, Heralds a New Life of Wonder

In July 2014, I finally took the biggest leap of faith in my life. I resigned from the bank leaving behind twenty two years of flourishing banking and solid financial security. It was a major switch that shocked many people. Banking is one of the highest paid industries in Sri Lanka. Anyone who takes a drastic step like I did, for the cause of a dream, is considered a raving lunatic!

I lost sixty five percent of my take home gratuity and retirement benefits. With all that I stand strong, for today I am proud of my decision. I have finally given myself the long awaited opportunity of going out into the world, educating and inspiring people to find a better way to live their lives.

Immediately after I bid goodbye to the banking industry, I started on a long awaited journey that I had kept on hold for a few years; a journey towards becoming a Napoleon Hill Foundation certified instructor. I took the home study course, the spring 2015 Distance Learning Course and finally the Leader Certification Course in March 2015 in French Lick, Indiana.

The class in French Lick was the most amazing experience of my life. I had been looking forward to being a part of this class since 2012 and finally achieved it in 2015. My life will never be the same again. I hope, because of my experience, many more people's lives will also change forever. The learning, sharing and growing was enormous. March 2015 has been a magical month for me, because I spent time with so many wonderful people, who are all students and instructors of the philosophy taught by Dr. Napoleon Hill.

Taking this class has opened the doors for me, to be a part of an incredible mastermind group, with, Napoleon Hill Foundation Certified Instructors from around the world. We meet regularly to mastermind our success by sharing insights, generating great ideas and inspiring each other, to tap into the infinite abundance that exists within ourselves. Connecting and interacting with like-minded people, who all testify to the myriad benefits the **Seventeen Principles** have brought into their lives, is proof indeed, that these are **Universal Laws** that actually work, and could be used by anybody, to uplift themselves out of poverty and misery. This mastermind group has brought into my life, countless wonders, that I could never have achieved all by myself. This is true and applicable to every human being, who desires to rise above mediocrity and soar high in life. Such is the power of a mastermind alliance!

All Who Succeed in Life Get Off to a Bad Start

I launched **"SuccessMind Global"**, my own Executive Development and Performance Coaching business in October 2014, after giving up the security and prestige of an executive position in a banking job, I held for twenty-two years. Instead, I opted for the tough life of an entrepreneur, starting all over from scratch, in an entirely different field, because I wanted to make a difference in the world, and be counted for the contributions I make.

I have to admit that life has not been easy. I have encountered more setbacks than I ever anticipated. I started off my entrepreneurial life by getting into a negative mastermind alliance, which destroyed my finances, peace of mind and chances of achieving my long anticipated dream. The negative influences of this alliance lingered on for several months, and I was engulfed in a vicious web of negativity and despair. All those months, I lived in a dark tunnel, mentally paralyzed, and unable to see things clearly or positively. After much heartbreak, I realized that I needed to close the door to the past completely, and move forward with a positive mental attitude and strong spiritual faith. I realized that if I am able to put the past behind, then the future would be brighter for me. This powerful thought saved me from permanent disaster and brought my life back on track. Very slowly, I was able to finally come out of the miserable black tunnel, and into the light of hope and positivity.

After my disastrous debut as an entrepreneur, and the subsequent lesson I learned about being careful with whom I share my dreams with, I thought things would change and life would move on smoothly. But I was in for more nasty surprises. I continued to face many obstacles and defeats along my entrepreneurial journey, including financial losses due to my *'uncontrolled enthusiasm'* to serve and my *'eagerness'* to live my dream. Lessons in life I learned at a very high cost. *'Every defeat has a seed of an equivalent or greater benefit'* and it is up to us to discover and benefit from it. I certainly have!

I am living my new life as a business owner, experiencing the many ups and downs any dream chaser is bound to undergo. Like in any new venture, my own dream venture has been slow in picking up business. Like every new entrepreneur, I am also on a roller-coaster ride, striving to make my business a success. Yet, I live with contentment today, because I know the **Seventeen Principles of Success** that I diligently practice, will guide me towards great achievement in life. The joy of seeing people escape the bonds of mediocrity, finding the courage to fight their self-imposed limitations, and striving to become extraordinary is worth its weight in gold.

I read **'Think & Grow Rich'** regularly, and each time, I learn something new that helps me to re-direct my journey to success on to the right path, just like all the others who accumulated abundant riches and worthy accomplishments by reading, re-reading and comprehending the important principles taught in this book. As a result of opening my mind to the wisdom taught by Dr. Hill, and conscientiously practicing his teachings, things are slowly beginning to turn brighter for my business and me. Innovative and exciting ideas are being explored to make the comeback journey a celebration. The future months hold plenty of hope and promises for me, because it's time to reap the benefits of my consistent and unwavering efforts.

AN ORDINARY RIVER TRANSFORMED INTO A POWERFULLY FLOWING RIVER

Looking back at the past few months, and the events that occurred during this time, I realize that life is like a rotating wheel, full of ups and downs. When good times come by, it will occasionally be replaced by bad times as well. Life would never be enjoyable and fruitful if we had positive experiences all the time. Dr. Napoleon Hill compares this life wheel to a great river. In his words, *"one half of this river flows in one direction and carries all who enter it to success, while the other half flows in the opposite direction and carries all who enter it to failure and defeat".* Dr. Hill calls this the **'River of Life'**, which *"exists in the power of human thought and dwells in the mind of man".* Mastering the **Seventeen Principles** of the **'Science of Success Philosophy'** provides the means by which one may cross from the failure side of the river to the success side.

Negative experiences, disappointments and adversity can teach us many invaluable lessons about ourselves, about the people we closely associate with, and about life. It may remove the blindfold away from our eyes, and reveal the truth to us. Sometimes the truths that are so revealed are not pleasant but, it will save us from misery and set things right. The most poignant moment, is when *'we'* stand before us, revealing our *'other side'* – the mighty, wise, spiritual side of us that is a huge powerhouse of internal strength and resilience, enough to sustain us through the biggest heart-wrenching failures in our lives. I have seen *'that side'* of me which is why I am so confident that very soon it will be my time to shine.

Life never gives us trials and tribulations with the intention of crushing and destroying us. To the contrary, it wants us to earn its rewards and blessings by proving ourselves. Just like we want the 'best man' to win in a game, life too wants the 'best man' to win. However, we will be tested before being rewarded, and passing the test is the toughest part of the game called life. Many fail this test miserably. As tough as life's lessons most often are, each carries with it the *'seed of an equivalent or greater benefit'* and a direction towards positive growth as a truly blessed human being. It is our responsibility to learn and profit from each lesson life teaches us, for our own benefit. Learning from adversity and defeat, and emerging victorious is the only way of proving, that we are fit for the rewards that life has to offer for the **'winners'**. As a humble victor in the game of life, I can sum up my own journey from failure to success as a simple but profound truth; *"the essence of my defeats and failures is that it is very much a part of my ultimate success."*

Even though I have had to face setbacks in my entrepreneurial journey, studying this philosophy and, comprehending its essence, has made me realize that I was right in making this change - the change in my career and the change in direction. I have proved not only to myself, but also, to many others who endorse my decision, that I am finally on my way to living the life I was created to live.

I have been blessed with talents that would never be useful in a banking career. Therefore, I believe that my new direction in life is the perfect execution of a divine plan. Today, I am living the life I have always dreamt of, by devoting time to a *'labor of love'* as Dr. Hill puts it. Analyzing the defeats faced by me, I am now able to find the *'seed of an equivalent benefit'*. I have a clear idea of where I was wrong, and what actions led to them. I see myself as a river flowing through obstacles and setbacks, becoming stronger and more powerful along the way, and I will reach my destination just like a river naturally would.

I would have never understood the deep wisdom behind my life experiences, had I not studied the **Seventeen Principles** of the **'Science of Success Philosophy'**. Close scrutiny of my life journey signifies to me that, I am very much on the success side of the **'River of Life'** but it will take a while more for the world to notice it. This philosophy will help me to become a *'lighthouse'* for all those people I personally know who have the potential, but are afraid to take control of their mind.

My Childhood Dreams Are Achieved After All!

When Mother Nature gives us talents, she also gives us an opportunity to use them. One good thing the setbacks in my life has done to me, is that they have re-ignited another childhood passion that was slain years ago; my passion for creative writing. I have started to write again. A few of my writings have been published and appreciated by my readers. And now, I am halfway through writing my first book - a parable for success that could be enjoyed by anyone irrespective of their age, if they savor an enchanting story, packed with inspiration to soar high in life. Writing this book is the **'BUTTERFLY MOMENT'** that I have been long anticipating, which has made my life worth living.

Along with my teaching profession, my writing profession has also taken off thanks to the **"thinking"** I was forced to do during the past few months. Finally, I am living my passion; my purpose in life! I believe that some of the best things in life cannot be planned; They just happen according to a mysteriously divine direction - just like the realization of cherished dreams.

"Nature never takes anything away from anyone without replacing it with something better" - carefully analyzing the setbacks and defeats in my

own life proves that there is a world of truth behind this statement. Because of all the adversities I have had to face, it has turned the course of my life in an entirely different path. I have come to recognize the spiritual forces that are leading me towards a bigger and better direction, where I can serve the world and make it a better place. It is an exciting and promising path because I can already visualize the beautiful, vivid and fragrant flower buds adorning the two sides. Each bud resembles my grandest dreams in life. The priceless lessons learned along the journey and the infinite benefits derived from these lessons, signify hope for me - that the flower buds have already begun to blossom.

The spring distance learning course and the leader certification course I took have been responsible for re-kindling my childhood dreams, and setting them on fire again. I am very grateful for that. I believe that I was sent here on earth to serve humanity, using the innate talents I was born with; to empower and inspire others to live their best life, and that is my purpose in life. Come what may, I will persist, standing strong on the wings of my dreams!

As I pen the last few lines of this chapter, my phone keeps ringing, repeatedly interrupting my writing. The calls are from prospective participants for my upcoming workshop on communication skills development, scheduled to be held in a week's time. There were seven registrations today alone! I am confident that my workshop would be sold-out by the time registration closes. As I ponder over the events of the past few months, I realize that I have discovered much more than a 'seed' of an equivalent benefit in my journey of transformation. I now fully understand and appreciate the divine direction in my life, and I am in harmony with the **Universe** and all the abundance it has in store for me.

I hope everybody who reads this chapter will be inspired to discover and live their purpose in life, burn all bridges behind them to follow their heart and make their journey along the **'River of Life'** a resounding success.

"Awake, arise, and assert yourself, you dreaners of the world. Your star is now in ascendancy."

-NAPOLEON HILL- THINK AND GROW RICH

Bio

Shadiya Zackaria is a Napoleon Hill Foundation Certified Instructor, with a tenacious vision of transforming ordinary people into extraordinary leaders by helping them discover their life purpose and maximize their potential, in living an abundant life. To make her vision a reality, she founded **SuccessMind Global (Pvt) Limited**, an organization specializing in Executive Training and Performance Coaching.

A committed professional with extensive experience and a sound track record in executive development, she serves the world as a Certified Professional Trainer, Life Coach, Hypnotherapist, Motivational Speaker and Creative Writer, sharing her rich life experiences, priceless lessons learned and personal triumphs to empower and inspire her clients to powerfully move forward in their own journey of transformation. She also serves as a Communication Skills Coach and is a Distinguished Toastmaster and a senior member of her home club, Wattala Toastmasters Club (Toastmasters International, USA). A dynamic Toastmaster leader, she has held the prestigious positions of Area Governor, Assistant Division Governor for Education & Training and is currently the Assistant Director for Program Quality in Division F - District 82.

She can be reached via e-mail at - shadiya@successmindglobal.com or company website www.successmindglobal.com or connect with her on LinkedIn - https://lk.linkedin.com/pub/shadiya-zackaria-5000-plus-connections/34/4a0/259.

BUILDING A SOLID SPIRITUAL FOUNDATION THAT WILL NEVER FAIL YOU

By Taylor Tagg

"Nature yields her most profound secrets to the person who is determined to uncover them."

- NAPOLEON HILL

ONE OF THE questions that arise often with clients is, "How can keep the events of my life from further frustrating me?"

One tried and true way is to examine the spiritual foundation on which you build your thoughts, ideas, and actions.

One great question to begin with is, "What do I stand for?"

"What lies underneath the decisions I make?"

Your spiritual foundation is something concrete to fall back on when events and situations get nasty in life. At the very minimum, your foundation will have three components of higher backing that will help you deal with any circumstance that comes your way.

I never thought I would find a way through a 30-year journey of childhood trauma, but I did. (detailed in the book *The Path to a Peaceful Heart*) It was my spiritual foundation that never let me fall completely away. It always held me up in a huge bind.

There are three virtues that can form the base of the foundation that guides your life. They are Faith, Hope, and Love.

We might know them today as Service (Love), Inspiration (Hope), and Trust (Faith) (SIT).

60

This terrific trio is what I call the SIT Principle for Heart Centered Living. By utilizing these virtues, you can SIT back to lead forward, which means use less effort to get more out of life. Let life work for you instead of the other way around. Let's look at how to do it.

#1 - Service, a form of Love, is the starting point for a spiritual foundation. Since Love is the most powerful emotion at your disposal, it will be the anchor that holds everything else up. When you commit to a mindset of service in your work, family life, and other areas something magical happens.

You are able to gain a sense of humility and gratitude while maintaining full power in everything you do. This combination is a package of spiritual balance which focuses on meeting your needs through helping others first.

When you approach your work in this way, service comes back to you in multiple arenas. Dr. Hill would say "serve yourself by serving others first." When you do, you activate that part of you that connects with others and through that connection you get what you need.

Nurses, accountants, speakers, garbage collectors, and people from all walks of life can choose to serve others in their work. As they do, they find definiteness of purpose, which Dr. Hill called "the starting point of all achievement."

When you adopt a give first philosophy in life, it comes back to you in folds. We are all subject to the natural law of reaping what we sow, good or not. Make your harvest count by serving others first in whatever you are called to do in your life. Your spiritual foundation will become solid, able to bear the weight of everything else that is to come your way.

#2 - The second virtue that builds upon Service is Inspiration. Inspiration, a form of Hope, is the joy and promise that you can bring to all facets of life and the people you meet. Inspiration is a belief of something better to come, brought about by a thought or word that is positive.

Simply telling someone they are amazing can be unbelievably inspiring. Try it and be prepared for a surprisingly positive reaction in return.

Have you ever noticed that people are attracted to those that make them feel good about themselves? We long to build connections with others that go beneath the surface. Inspiring someone else just by giving them a heartfelt compliment goes a long way in building relationships with others and making your own spiritual foundation solid.

Let's look at the word inspiration. The term can be broken down into two words – In Spirit.

In Spirit entails coming from a higher place within that is greater than you the human being. It's affirming, contributing, supporting, and loving. When one is In Spirit, he or she rises above fear, sees the good in others, and activates the Spirit in others. As one becomes more In Spirit, Spirit rebounds back to you in all kinds of fantastic ways.

When I was down in the dumps over losing a relationship that I cared deeply about, I had the thought that giving my time away to a cause would be good distraction so I wouldn't have to think about the end of the romance. I volunteered my time at a soup kitchen, feeding the homeless and hungry with peanut butter and jelly sandwiches.

I talked with many of them and offered words of encouragement for their journeys. On my way home, I turned off the radio in the car to reflect on the day and suddenly the end of my romance didn't seem so important. Here I was with people that didn't have access to a good meal, and I was worried about how I was going to get my girlfriend back. I saw that what I thought was important was not important at all. I would be ok. I got In Spirit by giving my time to feeding others and that experience gave me the gift of a higher perspective. My focus quickly went to how I could give more.

"Perhaps we shall learn, as we pass through this age,
that the 'other self" is more powerful than the physical
self we see when we look into a mirror."

- Napoleon Hill.

#3 - Trust, a form of Faith, is the ability to rely on others to help you meet your needs in due time. Trust is the direct opposite of control. Trust is the process of surrendering to a higher intelligence knowing that your intentions will be met at the right time. Trust allows for space to receive instead of attempting to direct every portion of the outcome. When you Trust, trust comes back to you in many reaffirming ways.

Faith is that belief that everything has its place in nature. Nature has a prevalent order to it. The stars, the cosmos have a distinct pattern that is followed without exception.

To build a solid spiritual foundation, we must activate faith in our own pattern of growth in life. We have the power to choose our path, to set out intentions of what we desire for our life and our legacy. But then faith must prevail and we have to get out of our own way and allow that growth to happen!

All in all, the virtues of Service, Inspiration, and Trust are designed to help you build a solid base beneath your feet. You might fall, but you will always have the ability to get up because your foundation is supporting you all the while.

When you get in situations of continual frustration and suffering, it's usually because one of these virtues of service, inspiration, or trust in lacking in your life.

Ask, how can I serve this troublesome thing, inspire the person who is at odds with me, or trust that this situation will work out for the best?

Direct your thoughts and actions to building a solid spiritual foundation to support you. Knowing that all the decisions you make are in concert with higher principles that are always working in your favor gives you permission to courageously stand and face any circumstance that comes your way.

Let life will work for you instead of happen to you. Less effort will be rewarded with greater results because you set your intentions and allowed them to arrive on time.

Adopt a philosophy of serving others through your work, inspiring them by being In Spirit, and activating faith that your life has an order that will unfold in your best interest.

Sometimes, the best thing you can do is to SIT back to move forward.

Building a Solid Spiritual Foundation That Will Never Fail You

"Nature yields her most profound secrets to the person who is determined to uncover them."

- NAPOLEON HILL

One of the questions that arises often with clients is,

"How can keep the events of my life from further frustrating me?"

One tried and true way is to examine the spiritual foundation on which you build your thoughts, ideas, and actions.

One great question to begin with is,

"What do I stand for?"

"What lies underneath the decisions I make?"

Your spiritual foundation is something concrete to fall back on when events and situations get nasty in life. At the very minimum, your foundation will have three components of higher backing that will help you deal with any circumstance that comes your way.

I never thought I would find a way through a 30 year journey of childhood trauma, but I did. (detailed in the book *The Path to a Peaceful Heart*) It was my spiritual foundation that never let me fall completely away. It always held me up in a huge bind.

There are three virtues that can form the base of the foundation that guides your life. They are Faith, Hope, and Love.

We might know them today as Service (Love), Inspiration (Hope), and Trust (Faith) (SIT).

This terrific trio is what I call the SIT Principle for Heart Centered Living. By utilizing these virtues, you can SIT back to lead forward, which means use less effort to get more out of life. Let life work for you instead of the other way around. Let's look at how to do it.

#1 - Service, a form of Love, is the starting point for a spiritual foundation. Since Love is the most powerful emotion at your disposal, it will be the anchor that holds everything else up. When you commit to a mindset of service in your work, family life, and other areas something magical happens.

You are able to gain a sense of humility and gratitude while maintaining full power in everything you do. This combination is a package of spiritual balance which focuses on meeting your needs through helping others first.

When you approach your work in this way, service comes back to you in multiple arenas. Dr. Hill would say "serve yourself by serving others first." When you do, you activate that part of you that connects with others and through that connection you get what you need.

Nurses, accountants, speakers, garbage collectors, and people from all walks of life can choose to serve others in their work. As they do, they find definiteness of purpose, which Dr. Hill called "the starting point of all achievement."

When you adopt a give first philosophy in life, it comes back to you in folds. We are all subject to the natural law of reaping what we sow, good or not. Make your harvest count by serving others first in whatever you are called to do in your life. Your spiritual foundation will become solid, able to bear the weight of everything else that is to come your way.

#2 - The second virtue that builds upon Service is Inspiration. Inspiration, a form of Hope, is the joy and promise that you can bring to all facets of life and the people you meet. Inspiration is a belief of something better to come, brought about by a thought or word that is positive.

Simply telling someone they are amazing can be unbelievably inspiring. Try it and be prepared for a surprisingly positive reaction in return. Have you ever noticed that people are attracted to those that make them feel good about themselves? We long to build connections with others that go beneath the surface. Inspiring someone else just by giving them a heartfelt compliment goes a long way in building relationships with others and making your own spiritual foundation solid.

Let's look at the word inspiration. The term can be broken down into two words – In Spirit.

In Spirit entails coming from a higher place within that is greater than you the human being. It's affirming, contributing, supporting, and loving. When one is In Spirit, he or she rises above fear, sees the good in others, and activates the Spirit in others. As one becomes more In Spirit, Spirit rebounds back to you in all kinds of fantastic ways.

When I was down in the dumps over losing a relationship that I cared deeply about, I had the thought that giving my time away to a cause would be good distraction so I wouldn't have to think about the end of the romance. I volunteered my time at a soup kitchen, feeding the homeless and hungry with peanut butter and jelly sandwiches.

I talked with many of them and offered words of encouragement for their journeys. On my way home, I turned off the radio in the car to reflect on the day and suddenly the end of my romance didn't seem so important. Here I was with people that didn't have access to a good meal, and I was worried about how I was going to get my girlfriend back. I saw that what I thought was important was not important at all. I would be ok. I got In Spirit by giving my time to feeding others and that experience gave me the gift of a higher perspective. My focus quickly went to how I could give more.

"Perhaps we shall learn, as we pass through this age,
that the 'other self" is more powerful than the physical
self we see when we look into a mirror."

-NAPOLEON HILL.

#3 - Trust, a form of Faith, is the ability to rely on others to help you meet your needs in due time. Trust is the direct opposite of control. Trust is the process of surrendering to a higher intelligence knowing that your intentions will be met at the right time. Trust allows for space to receive instead of attempting to direct every portion of the outcome. When you Trust, trust comes back to you in many reaffirming ways.

Faith is that belief that everything has its place in nature. Nature has a prevalent order to it. The stars, the cosmos have a distinct pattern that is followed without exception.

To build a solid spiritual foundation, we must activate faith in our own pattern of growth in life. We have the power to choose our path, to set out intentions of what we desire for our life and our legacy. But then faith must prevail and we have to get out of our own way and allow that growth to happen!

All in all, the virtues of Service, Inspiration, and Trust are designed to help you build a solid base beneath your feet. You might fall, but you will always have the ability to get up because your foundation is supporting you all the while.

When you get in situations of continual frustration and suffering, it's usually because one of these virtues of service, inspiration, or trust in lacking in your life.

Ask, how can I serve this troublesome thing, inspire the person who is at odds with me, or trust that this situation will work out for the best?

Direct your thoughts and actions to building a solid spiritual foundation to support you. Knowing that all the decisions you make are in concert with higher principles that are always working in your favor gives you permission to courageously stand and face any circumstance that comes your way.

Let life will work for you instead of happen to you. Less effort will be rewarded with greater results because you set your intentions and allowed them to arrive on time.

Adopt a philosophy of serving others through your work, inspiring them by being In Spirit, and activating faith that your life has an order that will unfold in your best interest.

Sometimes, the best thing you can do is to SIT back to move forward.

Taylor Tagg is a published author, professional speaker, and podcast host. He has written three personal development books, *Enrich Your*

Sunrise, The Path to a Peaceful Heart, and Adversity to Advantage. Taylor's podcast, *Journey to Success,* showcases people who are passionate about making a difference in the world with transformational businesses and ideas. Taylor's natural talent lies in coaching people in how to fulfill their emotional and spiritual potential. A Spiritual Empowerment Coach and Emotional Intelligence Expert, Taylor helps those dealing with significant adversity to walk the path to peace using his proven process. He lives in Memphis, Tennessee with his wife Sherri. http://www. theevolvingheart.com/

Bio

Taylor Tagg is a published author, professional speaker, and radio show host. He has written two personal growth books, *Enrich Your Sunrise* and *The Path to a Peaceful Heart.* Taylor's BlogTalk radio show, *Journey to Success,* showcases people who are passionate about making a difference in the world with transformational businesses and ideas. Taylor's natural talent lies in coaching people in how to fulfill their emotional and spiritual potential. A Forgiveness Coach and Emotional Intelligence Expert, Taylor empowers those dealing with significant adversity to aspire to peace using his proven process. He lives in Memphis, Tennessee with his wife Sherri. http://www.theevolvingheart.com/

Living Within The Affirmation

By Colin Gilmartin

Why do you, Colin Gilmartin, have three felony arrests in an eight-month period? Asked a judge with the Superior Court in New Hampshire, March 1991.

"I don't know." I replied. My only truth at that moment was three words. And since I did not know why, I could not make a change.

Thus followed enrollment in the *Shock Incarceration* program at New Hampshire State Prison where I met Napoleon Hill—not *literally*, but literature-ly, and the seeds of achievement were planted and watered regularly with comprehension.

According to Scholastic.com, *"It is not until the age of 7, give or take a year or so, that your child's conscience begins to mature enough to guide her actions."*

When we were babies we interpreted the actions and tones of our surroundings. Until we associated definitions to words, and further ascribed to semantics, we interpreted at a deeper level. Our minds were open to all ideas. ALL ideas: negative and positive. The connections we made through association with those influencing our lives, combined with our genetic drives, shaped us into preschoolers, teenagers and adults. We reached an age of reason; each with a unique set of values.

Looking back, I know there were abundant negative associations in my childhood, and unlike mathematics—wherein two negatives multiply to make a positive—my foundation was set.

"There can be no positive outcome from a negative idea."

—Napoleon Hill.

The power of repeated demonstration is exampled in the simplicity of brushing one's teeth compared to the outcome of not doing so; profound is the influence of the demonstrator of this twice a day routine.

As a parent squeezes the paste onto the brush then mimics the up-and-down strokes, tooth brushing becomes a positive habit; as close to an intrinsic behavior as one can get.

And so, every idea presented by those closest to us—especially when we are young—is filtered, evaluated, and tucked away inside each developing cell—ultimately fixed in subconscious.

I used to hear, "You're just like your father." The statement of the day often modeled a version of, "You make me so angry." Sometimes the latter was directed at me, other times someone else. The point is I inhaled every destructive ion.

Hearing people disagree or listening to them complain about limitations is as tragic—and effective—as permanent ink on linen.

I must have had the ability to think and reason by the time I was seven, but my actions told a different tale. Chapter by chapter I created a story from the history of others, for that is how all life-books are written.

All messages stick and bleed to form the foundation of a child's belief system.

To counter any doubt over the 'stickability' of words—which form messages—which become beliefs—one only has to recount seasonal jingles. The *Baby Alive* lullaby or the *Popomatic Trouble* rhyme. If COKE could teach the world to sing, think of the harmonies that were daily scores in dysfunctional households. No amount of 'I am stuck on Bandaid' can cover that wound.

And so returns the judge's question. Why?

Because although I blamed others for what was happening in my environment—it was never my responsibility—the truth was that I never understood myself. What others saw as 'problems' I saw as being me. And I was 'being me' for a quite a while until Napoleon Hill introduced that 'me' to this 'me'.

Beyond the incredible capacity with which we are born—to think— many of us are programmed for negative thought.

Dr. Ken McFarline says *"2% of people think, 3% think they think, and the other 95% would rather die than think."*

No wonder some of us have an aversion to thinking, given our thought patterns have not been modeled on joy. Perhaps it is self-preservation not to ponder, ruminate, or analyze. It's just too painful.

In many cases the people who create us, even though they love us the best they can (with the skills they have), hack into the hardwiring of an open mind and plant serious viruses. Though unintentional, their brand of 'thoughtlessness' corrupts our own.

There's a deep rut that runs along the path of poor influence— one containing the footprints of many children who are following those formed by the size tens of their 'leaders'.

The demonstration of positive through words and actions will provide a fork in that road—a route to greatness, as it did for me.

One of the most outstanding aspects of human behavior is that we can see the physical growth of a young person, but unless you are a trained mechanic and look under the hood—ask the right questions—there is no way of knowing that child's emotional intelligence.

One of the ways I condition my mind today is through the repetition of affirmations. "I AM happy and grateful to share Napoleon Hill's philosophy of individual achievement to every school-aged child who wants and needs it."

In the end, I AM thinking.

Bio

What do you get when you combine Napoleon Hill's philosophy with the theatrics of Dr. Seuss? You get Colin Gilmartin. Every morning this nationally ranked coach greets his purpose: making a difference. It wasn't always that way—Coach G. is proof of life's meaningful U-turns. His leadership goes beyond athletics in facilitating access to greatness for kids.

Colin has a BA in Criminal Justice and two MBA's; one in Finance/Accounting and the second in International Business. Colin pursues his passion as a professional coach while working and playing in the great city of New Orleans. He has recently authored a bestselling book called Dream Training – A Practical Guide for Today's Youth to Achieve Their Dreams through Lifestyle Entrepreneur Press. He has a USSF "A" License Colin is also finishing up his requirements to become a Napoleon Hill Instructor.

He currently coaches and teaches youngsters at the Louisiana Fire Soccer club of New Orleans. His dream is to deliver 75,000 Dream Training books to every 8-14 year old in the city of New Orleans.

Colin Gilmartin, Author of Dream Training – A Practical Guide for Today's Youth to Achieve Their Dreams.

The Power Of A Definite Major Purpose

By Eduard Lopez

Definite Major Purpose. Life purpose. Life's main objective. Life's dreams. There are so many different ways to express the same concept.

We have heard countless times about the importance of having a definite purpose in life, although most of the population does not have one. What exactly is a Definite Major Purpose? Napoleon Hill describes it as the "starting point of all achievement". Without knowing what you want, it's going to be impossible to achieve it. That's why we should decide what our purpose is early in life, and dedicate all of our thoughts and actions to achieving it.

But why aren't we doing this? Why is 98% of the population, when asked, not able to explain their purpose in life? There are many different reasons.

One is timing.

When someone decides to set up a goal large enough to be considered his Definite Major Purpose in life, there's an expectation that it will take the greater part of his life to achieve it. And we know that the many different circumstances that a person faces in his or her life will distract, frustrate, and discourage the ability to persist in achieving this purpose.

It takes a lot of determination, persistence, self-discipline, focus, cooperation with others, and faith.

In *Think and Grow Rich*, Napoleon Hill describes the steps required to achieve whatever we want, or our Definite Major Purpose, allowing us to understand what we need to do. Most of us have discovered Dr. Hill's work after spending so many years of our lives without a clearly defined purpose. And still, many people continue without one.

My question is: if having a Definite Major Purpose is so important to our life's achievements, what happens to those of us who have spent a large part of our lives without a clear purpose, or without conscious knowledge of what we want to achieve? Can we accomplish something in life without knowing or deciding what we want to achieve? In the early days, after I read Napoleon Hill's work for the second time, I was fully convinced that I knew the answer: we cannot achieve anything if we do not know what we want to achieve. It seemed so obvious.

I thought about my life and, eventually, I saw things a bit differently. I understood then about the power of a Definite Major Purpose and what happens if you do not clearly identify what you want.

I come from a family whose early years were based on a struggle to get ahead. My father was enrolled in the army for 18 months, back when Spain still had a military conscription policy. After his mandatory service, he took on several menial jobs until he finally joined my grand-father who managed a modest shop selling fabrics in a small town. The profits were small and the future wasn't overly promising.

My mother migrated with her family from the Spanish countryside to a location near a larger industrial area and began looking for jobs. Without any basic education, she was only able to find a job painting wall tiles by hand, working six days a week, 10 hours a day. She gave her wages to her mother to help sustain the family.

After my parents were married, my mother left that job and devoted her time to raising me and my brother and managing the house, sup-porting my father as he worked to develop that small shop, which pro-vided the only household income. All of my close relatives were more or less experiencing the same lifestyle: low income jobs, a lack of basic education, and living within their limitations.

It was in this environment where I frequently heard about the impor-tance of having security in life. It was years later before I realized that the comments and advice from everyone around me always emphasized the need to create a secure environment, save for a "rainy day", and be conscious of spending habits. This could only be achieved through sacrifice, study and finding a job in a solid "company".

I heard this message again and again throughout my early years.

I never really decided what I was going to do or be in life, but all of these comments were subconsciously resonating with me and shaping my reality.

My parents' sacrifice and a life of frugality allowed them to save enough money to send me to college. They did not have an education and wanted to provide their children with this opportunity. I completed a Masters degree in Engineering and began looking for jobs with companies that provide a solid future. After a few job interviews in the late 1980s, I was hired by IBM which, at that time, was one of the more 'secure' companies.

After getting married, and without a clear definite purpose, I found myself following in my parents' footsteps. I was only concerned with saving as much as I could, living a very simple life and only being worried about "what if" situations that could expose my family to financial risk. In the mid-'90s IBM decided to close or sell most of their manufacturing facilities and there was a risk that I would lose my job. I moved on to two other multinational companies, not as "safe" as IBM but the most secure businesses that I could find in the area.

In the pursuit of developing myself and gaining more experience, I decided to take an international assignment in two different countries for a total of nine years. It meant being away from my family but maintaining" safe" employment. Though I received very interesting offers from other companies, some which would lead to changes in my professional career path, I always decided that it was better to stay with my current company where I was still discovering opportunities for advancement.

After several years, *Think and Grow Rich* fell back into my hands but I had to read it twice to truly understand the essence of Napoleon Hill's philosophy. That's when I began realizing the importance of having a

Definite Major Purpose in life if I wanted to achieve something of significance. But first I had to discover my Definite Major Purpose in life. It was not an easy process. I realized that I had been working hard — trying to live a modest life and saving for the future — so my two daughters would have the same opportunities I had, and be able to attend college and find secure jobs. But beyond that, I could not find a specific purpose.

I realized that throughout my life, I had been following a definite but subconscious purpose in life that had been set up by my parents, by my environment and through social influences, but not by me. And, on top of it, it had been defined in negative terms; I was avoiding risk.

This is what I did for my entire life. I avoided risk as a means of providing the safest environment for my family so we would never suffer due to lack of money. I was not looking for any significant achievement, or any inspiring vision prompted by an amazing dream, or any accomplishment that would impact other people and help to improve the world. No, I was simply being safe by avoiding risk. This is what I unconsciously did for most of my life.

So now I come back to the earlier question: what is the power of a Definite Major Purpose?

A Definite Major Purpose guides your actions throughout your entire life. Consciously or unconsciously, you will always follow the path laid out by your major purpose. It will get you there, sooner or later.

I have another question that can dramatically change your life. Which is best: following a definite purpose that has been put in your subconscious mind by other people or by your environment, or deciding what you really want to achieve in life and putting it in front of you every day as a motivator?

Both scenarios can work. Unfortunately, the majority of the population doesn't realize this or, even when aware of the options, don't take their path in life seriously. Instead, they feel that their purpose is just a series of hopes and dreams, letting the environment around them dictate their actions and decisions.

Dr. Hill discovered this by studying the lives of more than 500 successful men worldwide during the first part of the 20th century. All of those men achieved extraordinary things by beginning with a Definite Major Purpose and following through until they achieved it.

Why shouldn't we do the same? Why leave our lives to chance rather than defining what we really want, writing it down, committing it to memory and relaying it through repetition of thought to our subconscious mind? If we do not do it, others will do it for us, and we will not take control of our actions and, therefore, our results in life.

The power of this principle is so strong that it's worth giving it a second thought and then implementing it. The reward will be waiting for you. I did it. I followed Dr. Hill's advice and I identified my purpose in life, wrote about it, committed it to memory and I'm repeating it daily.

After a short time amazing things started happening to me, both on the inside and outside. These were happenings, circumstances, encounters and coincidences that I could have never imagined when my only "purpose" was to avoid risk and look for safety.

A sense of optimism, a positive mental attitude, confidence, energy, a desire to serve others, and focus are only a few of the benefits that I am experiencing ... and I'm excited about what it is going to follow.

Hopefully you will also follow this path. It's truly the path of the most successful people.

Eduard Lopez.

Bio

Eduard was born in a small town in Spain from a low-middle class family. Having his parents completed only basic schooling; they managed to be able to save for Eduard's University where he got the MSc degree in Engineering.

Eduard has developed his entire professional career in Multinational companies, from his early days when he joined IBM's ranks as a junior professional, right after College.

IBM's crisis in the 1990s opened a new world of challenges and opportunities where the real Professional and Personal growth started. Always part of big Corporations, succeeding in dynamic and challenging environments was only possible through sustained Peak Performance individuals and teams.

Considered as one of his best decisions in life, Eduard developed his career in three different countries, getting to know how to successfully integrate the cultural differences into team and individual performance.

Knowing how hard is developing a career without experienced advice and support, his Mission has become helping people to accelerate the process of getting what they want to achieve in life. Becoming a Certified Instructor of the Napoleon Hill Foundation has set up the base for the successful accomplishment of that Mission.

"Eduard has a distinct Customer focused and solution oriented attitude. This is an experience I had the pleasure to have multiple times during the years we worked together. As usual, business relationships demonstrate their real strength in difficult and demanding times. In my experience with Eduard and the team he leads, this strength of the relationship has been extraordinary good. Eduard managed to focus always on the facts to get out of difficult situations or to help me and my Customers with expedited analysis as fast as possible to the benefit of both of us. Thus I would like to express my explicit thankfulness to Eduard and his team!" (**Dieter Sieben.** Engineering Manager IBM Europe).

Email: elopezgimeno@gmail.com

   https://ro.linkedin.com/in/eduardlopez

   https://plus.google.com/+EduardLopezGimeno/posts

Work your Dream!

By Codruta Bala

"What the mind of man can conceive, and believe,
it can achieve."

Napoleon Hill

My origins...

I was born in the late 70's during a period of communism in Romania. My father worked in construction and my mom worked as cashier in a grocery store.

I am the eldest of 2 children and have a younger brother. My parents worked all day, including weekends, in order to provide us everything we needed during our childhood. I am very happy and grateful that I was born into my family. It is from them that I learned the principles that have guided me in life including; Respect, Trust, Faith, Persistence, Going the Extra Mile, Positive Mental Attitude, and having a Definite Purpose.

Neither of my parents have a University degree. They grew up in the countryside, where working the land were the main occupation, and were considered a necessity for living. They fought with the system they grew up in and had the courage to move to the big city, far away from their parents, to earn a better living.

My parents rented a room in a house and started their married life together. After 2 years I came into their lives. It was probably not the best timing for them, as they were working hard to survive, however I have felt all my life that my parents loved me and I grew up surrounded by love. Big love.

I grew up seeing my parents working hard for everything we had. I saw them working hard, starting very early in the morning and working until early evening. It was not easy to work in construction, which was my father's job. It was really hard work. After coming home from working a minimum of 12 hours a day, he went to school, as he wanted to continue his studies after he graduated from primary school in the village he was born. After all these evening classes he still had the energy and enthusiasm to come home and play with me, or wash my diapers late into the night after I fell asleep. And this happened day after day...it was a permanent "job".

"The starting point of all achievement is desire."

NAPOLEON HILL

I grew up learning by candlelight; as we only had electricity a few hours a day, same thing with the heating. In order to buy milk, we had to wake up early in the morning to get in line at 4:00 am to be sure to get some. Everything was rationed and not many things were available. During winters, which were colder back then than they are today, I wore three sweaters and a sheepskin. And I didn't give up learning. I wanted to do more than my parents did, and I had their full support. My parents wanted both of us to go to university and achieve more than what they did in life. In their view, having a university degree meant having more possibilities and opportunities.

"A goal is a dream with a deadline."

NAPOLEON HILL

Ever since I was a kid my Definite Purpose was to help people in need, and to be able to make a difference before I turned 30 years of age. I wanted to graduate from law school. I wanted to protect people in need by becoming a lawyer or judge. Justice and correctitude was a part of my life, and the way my character was formed, I gave the impression I would become a successful lawyer or judge.

APPLIED FAITH...RESPONSIBILITY AND ACCOUNTABILITY CAME VERY FAST AS I GREW UP...

My brother and I, spent all summers at our grandparents, which was a great experience for both of us. I was the oldest and had to take care of my younger brother all the time. I remember my parents passing this responsibility to me when they were left to return to our home and leaving us in our grandparents' capable hands.

One of the role models I had when I was a kid was my maternal grandfather. He was a very committed and loyal person and I got to witness that first hand. He taught me what it means to have a DEFINITE PURPOSE in life. In the evenings he would tell me stories from the war, and how and what helped him survive during those times. He often told me: "My dear, you have to know what you want to achieve in life and don't let anyone disturb you from it. There will be tough periods in life, when you would like to renounce, but do not give up. Remember this forever, after the rain, the sun will come and shine more brightly than before. Keep this in your mind and you will be successful. Do not forget to keep your humility and be yourself all the time. It is more important to sleep well at night than anything else." At that time I did not understand what he was saying, as I was still very young. I was 14 when he passed away and this affected me a lot. As the years passed, I realized what he was saying, and remember his words like it was yesterday.

I specifically remember one summer, when my parents were planning to visit some foreign countries close to ours, and they left us in the care of my father's parents, our grandparents. During that time, in the late 1980's, people were not allowed to travel freely wherever or whenever they wanted, so they had to ask the Authorities for permission, what took a long time. The government would not allow us to go as an entire family because we might defect and never return which is why it was impossible for us to join them. I was 9 and my brother was 6 at the time.

I remember those two weeks as if it were yesterday. It was not common to travel at the time and when it happened, the people usually decided to remain in the foreign country and defect to get away from communism and start a new life with new opportunities. Because of this, my grandparents were very scared that my parents would not come back. All the neighbors were gossiping that my brother and I would grow up with my grandparents as my parents would not come back until they could take us with them, perhaps many years later. I remember my brother crying when he heard the rumors. My grandmother even told us that we would remain with them and how hard that was going to be as they are old. Even though I was only 9 years old I was strong, telling her: "Grandma, I know my parents will come back to Romania. They will not give up on us for anything in the world. They love us a lot so do not worry". I was also encouraging my brother, as he really needed me. I was the one who took care of the family, and I took it very seriously. Each night I watched the stars from my window and prayed to have my parents back home as soon as possible. Something inside me knew that they would come back. I did not know it at the time that this was APPLIED FAITH. I just knew that this would happen and it did really happen.

Becoming a lawyer...

My dream, my definite purpose in life since I was a kid was to go to law school. This happened and it was really my first success being admitted to that University because there was a very big competition to be admitted. Not coming from a rich family was not important as long as I had studied hard to get in. I wanted my parents to be proud of me. I remember people who knew my parents asking them "How come your daughter was admitted to law school since you do not have the money to support this?". This stayed in my head and gave me the power to work even harder to show that personal success does not depend on money.

Human Resources...

During my University years I was going the extra mile in all my activities outside of classes. I knew that in order to succeed I had to do more and more and so I got involved in different projects including being part of a NGO, where I discovered my new career in human resources. Even though my initial dream, since childhood, was to become lawyer or judge, I realized after some years at university that I would not have been fulfilled with the profession, and not be able to impact many lives. So, at the age of 19, human resources became my DEFINITE PURPOSE. I enjoyed working with people and contributing to their development. I loved helping others and organizing development events where everybody could learn something, including myself.

After graduating from law school, I started to work in different positions in Human Resources. My purpose was to become a Human Resources Manager of a big organization before I turned 30. I knew it would not be easy. I knew there were many things to learn but this didn't scare me at all. I wanted this role in order to be able to contribute more to the development of others, to be able to change the organizational culture and make people feel respected at work.

> "Any idea, plan or purpose may be placed in the mind through repetition of thought."
>
> Napoleon Hill

I was hired as a successor to a Human Resources Manager role when I was 28. I was so happy for that. I thought my dream would become true sooner than I thought. I repeated it in my prayers every night for years. Finally, when it seemed to becoming closer and closer to reality, 3 months after I got hired, the Human Resources Manager, my manager, resigned and her boss did not believe that I was ready for the role and that I did not have enough experience in the industry to be promoted. I was destroyed. I worked so hard during those years and this was my chance. I thought "How come this happens to me? It can't be true." I thought I deserved that role. Frustration and disappointment filled my mind and soul. I did not trust others, or myself. I kept asking the Universe and my God why this happened to me. In my own eyes, I had done everything perfect.

"Not only can failure become a habit, the same applies
to poverty, worry and pessimism. Any state of mind,
positive or negative, becomes a habit the moment it
begins to dominate the mind."

NAPOLEON HILL

This disappointment caused me to change the company I was working with by moving to another town than the one I was born in and lived almost all my life. I accepted a lower position but in a bigger company, where I thought the possibilities for growth were higher. I surprised everybody with my decision. I analyzed what went well and wrong before and why my purpose in life was not met. And I started to focus on the future not the past any longer.

"Your big opportunity may be right where you are now."

NAPOLEON HILL

I was positively surprised when my previous company and the same person who considered I was not ready for the job previously, contacted me to offer me, after less than a year, the role I wanted. "Wow! This can't be true" I was telling myself. How come now, after less than a year I was ready for the job? What made me ready? Why now? Why me? I think there are moments in everybody's life when we should not question everything, which comes into our lives. I think everything comes at the right moment, when we are really ready for it and we should just be THANKFUL for what we receive.

> "Every time a man rises from defeat, he becomes mentally and spiritually stronger. Thus, in time, one may actually find himself – his true, inner self – through temporary defeat."

> Napoleon Hill

So I became a Human Resources Manager 5 months before I turned 30. It was like a dream come true. I realized now, after some years, that I was not ready for the role in the first place. I think I still needed time to learn from adversity and defeat. I needed time to learn from my mistakes. I needed time to mature myself and be ready. After a few years I was promoted to Human Resources Director, which was even more than what I initially set as my purpose.

> "Positive mental attitude is determined by you.
> Not others."

> Napoleon Hill

With my Definite Purpose, together with Applied Faith, I saw myself all the time in possession of my dream. Going the Extra Mile and Learning from Adversity and Defeat, gave me persistence and I have achieved my dream.

Learning Napoleon Hill's philosophies and the 17 success principles helped me a lot in life. I started to see things from a different perspective and worked hard to keep my positive mental attitude all the time. I know it is not easy when you go through defeat to keep your attitude positive. It is an ongoing fight not to think negatively, to look to the future and learn from any situation. You have to be aware of your state of mind all the time and continue working towards your definite purpose. Never give up. Great things are in front of you. You can make it. I trust that you will be successful in everything you do as long as you believe it as well.

> "Mental attitude controls, very largely, the space one occupies in life, the success one achieves, the friends one makes, and the contributions one makes to posterity. It would be no great overstatement of the truth if we said that mental attitude is EVERYTHING."

> NAPOLEON HILL

With love,
Codruta Bala

Bio

Codruta has 15+ years experience in human resources area that was accumulated by having different roles during her career in big multinational companies from IT, FMCG or EMS industries. She is passionate about personal development since she was a kid and the proof is all the training or seminars she attended during all these years and continues attending.

She is motivated by transforming the others in a better version of themselves which she continues doing it in her professional and also personal life. Her definite purpose in life is to change the world in a better one where people will be living their lives with Positive Mental Attitude and Going the Extra Mile in any situation, without expecting anything in exchange. She is involved in many social responsibility projects and was recognized as a pioneer in this area at regional and national level, being an example for the others around.

Her involving with the Napoleon Hill philosophy and coaching has given Codruta's work a different dimension to create an inspiring environment that can impact other people in their professional and personal lives.

"I work with HR Directors all over the world and Codruta Bala is the best of the best. She truly cares for her associates' well-being, corporate education and day-to-day satisfaction as team members. She has raw intelligence, is emotionally and socially intelligent and is a joy to work with. She is a learner, a leader and model for employees. I recommend her without reservation."

Jim Bagnola. President: The Leadership Group International

Email: codruta.bala@gmail.com
https://ro.linkedin.com/in/codrutabala

Why Wouldn't You?

By Chuck DeWayne

I WAS OFFICIALLY introduced to Napoleon Hill and his principles and philosophies in 2011. What I came to discover after my introduction was that I had been impacted by his philosophies and principles for many years. It is my pleasure to share a few experiences of how two of the principles of Napoleon Hill have impacted my life and the life of my family.

Definite Major Purpose

Napoleon Hill says that a Definite Major Purpose is the starting point for all personal achievement. He also states that a *Definite Major Purpose* is a stumbling block for ninety-seven out of one hundred people because they never really define or discover their *Definite Major Purpose* or develop any personal goals. The choice is yours. You can choose to be a victim of life or a victor in life.

In the Fall of 1977, I found my Definite Purpose, or rather the Universe found it for me. I had finished my core requirements for graduation but I needed another class my senior year in high school in order to graduate so I signed up to be a teacher's aide at a local elementary school. The minute I sat down and started working with those kids I was hooked. I knew right away that teaching was the profession I was destined to pursue. I spent nearly 50 years in education as a Student, Teacher, Principal, Director of Curriculum, Instruction & Assessment and finally, Executive Director of Human Resources. I dedicated most of my life to provide the best possible environment and education for what I consider our most precious resource, children. I had what many would consider an exemplary career. During my time in education I earned two Bachelor's Degrees, a Masters Degree and multiple certificates and licenses from four universities. Of all of the degrees, licenses and certifications I have earned, the one I consider the most valuable and the most powerful is the Leadership Certification I earned from the Napoleon Hill Foundation. My only regret is I didn't have that training when I began my career as an educator. The power and knowledge of the principles and philosophies of Napoleon Hill are skills that every student needs to prepare them to be successful adults. This is even truer in a world that is changing exponentially. The world today's kids are growing up in is definitely different than the one I grew up in.

I am blessed to have two beautiful daughters, Sydney, who will begin her junior in college and Charlie, who just graduated from high school. One of their favorite things is listening to stories from the "good old days" when my wife and I were their age. Some of you will be able to relate to these facts. They think it is hilarious that back in the day television had 4 channels and my sisters and I were the remote control, or the fact that my TV in college was black and white. They also think it is funny that I was so excited when Brother Typewriters came out with "memory" that would allow me to whiteout a few sentences of text. Of course they don't know what a typewriter is. They also still aren't sure if I am telling the truth that gas was 25 cents a gallon when I started to drive or that you could get a hamburger, fries and a coke and change back from your dollar at McDonald's.

Yes change is happening everywhere. Richard Friedman describes it as "The World is Flat" in his best-selling book by the same name. There are also numerous "Did You Know" videos available with some startling facts. For example: 3.5 zetabytes of new information (that's 3.5 with twenty 0's after it) will be created this year. That is more than the amount generated in the previous 5,000 years. The amount of new technical information is doubling every year. For students starting a four-year degree program this means that half of what they learn in their first year of college is outdated by their third year. The top 10 in-demand jobs in

2013 didn't exist in 2004. That means we are currently preparing kids for jobs that don't yet exist. The 25% of the population in China with the highest IQ's is greater than the total population of North America. In India the number is 28%. That means they have more honor kids than we have kids. The world population in 2013 reached 7 billion. According to a January 2014 story in Forbes Magazine, the 85 richest people in the world have as much wealth as the bottom 3.5 billion people. Put another way, 85 people have the combined wealth of ½ the world's population. I don't know about you but as a parent and educator these statistics make me stop and take notice.

Despite all of these changes the content we teach our kids is basically the same as it was when I began school in 1965. Yes the "how" has changed, from chalkboards to smart boards and iPads but the "what" has remained basically the same. That is no way a reflection on teachers. I hold teachers in the highest regard. I believe teaching is one of the toughest jobs in the world. If you don't believe me, try and take 25-40 kids from different backgrounds, ethnicities, skills, and languages and try to teach them academics and social skills. It is more a reflection on the system of education, and the political nature of education in the 21st Century. There is a long history of legislation at both the state and federal level that drive educational change. The amount of legislation has ramped up considerably since 2000. "No Child Left Behind", passed by a bipartisan coalition in Congress in 2002, marked a new direction. In exchange for more federal aid, the states were required to measure progress and punish schools that were not meeting the goals as measured by standardized state exams in math and language skills. While lawmakers were well intended, by 2012, half the states were given waivers because the original goal that 100% of students by 2014 be deemed "proficient" had proven unrealistic. Measuring all kids the same, no matter the type of diversity they come to school with, makes no more sense than going into a 4th grade classroom and telling them they all have to be the same height and weight. We give students the exact same test as though they have the exact same skills, language, experiences and backgrounds. By tying funding to performance in reading, writing and math it also squeezed out instruction in many other valuable contents. At the same time the push for 21st Century was gaining momentum in the private sector (http://www.p21.org/). All of this left teachers to wonder how they were going to teach everything with the high demands and limited time. After spending almost 50 years of my life in education I was becoming more and more frustrated with the politics surrounding education. Education is less and less about kids and more and more about cut scores, conformity and compliance.

In my school district, the Board of Education passed a new policy in alignment with the 21st Century Skills movement. At the time my job as Director of Curriculum, Instruction and Assessment was to make sure this policy was met. Mostly it was seen by our teachers as just one more thing they had to learn and squeeze into an already overly demanding list of things to teach kids. At the same time the state was revamping its state test's to align with these 21st Century concepts and to marry them with the required academics. As you can imagine, this is a lot for teachers and school districts to handle. Oh by the way, the economy was way down and funding was being cut across the nation.

In 2011 my wife went to work with Organo Gold, a company that was founded on and operates by the principles of Napoleon Hill's work, Think and Grow Rich, and his 17 Success Principles. Organo Gold has an exclusive and very coveted collaboration with the Napoleon Hill Foundation. This collaboration is signified by an Organo Gold Edition of Think and Grow Rich.

Shortly after Stephanie went to work with Organo Gold I attended some of her company's trainings. The trainings were based on personal development but more specifically on the philosophies and principles of Napoleon Hill. I was immediately drawn to the positive nature of his philosophies so I read Think & Grow Rich. It was like the proverbial light bulb coming on. The Principles in Think & Grow Rich and Dr. Hill's 17 Success Principles were the missing piece for education. These principles were what kids need to survive and thrive in today's world.

They aligned perfectly with our Board of Education's new policy. We had both of our kids read the book and start coming to the Saturday trainings. They too were hooked. Things were starting to align. Later that school year my oldest daughter Sydney, who was a junior in high school, was given an assignment to write about where she would be in 5 years. Using the Principle of Definite of Purpose, she wrote that in 5 years she would be a millionaire. This brought giggles from her classmates and her teacher. Her teacher told her she needed to write a realistic goal. Sydney said it is a realistic goal and in fact we have a family friend who is 23 and is a millionaire. A little more debate ensued and the teacher finally told her to write a realistic goal or get an "F" on the assignment. Bless my daughter's heart she believes that thoughts truly are things and told the teacher give me the F, it is a realistic goal. She came home and shared this story with myself and her mom. As parents, we were shocked and angry that a teacher would tell her this. As a member of the superintendent of schools cabinet and former director of curriculum and instruction I was flabbergasted. My first reaction was to drive over to the school to see the teacher. Thankfully, it was a Friday afternoon and I had the weekend to reflect on the interaction and to calm down. Over the weekend I had time to reflect and realized that it wasn't really the teacher's fault. It was a lack of understanding on her part and an illustration that not only aren't kids getting the teachings they need, neither are teachers. That weekend my Definite Major Purpose in life of being an educator shifted to include teaching the 17 Success Principles to not just students but also to staff.

Dr. Hill teaches that, as you gain a Definite Purpose in life and begin to take action, the Law of Attraction kicks in and opportunity follows. That came into play a short time later. As I was waiting for a meeting to begin, I was speaking to the Career and Tech Ed Coordinator who worked under me in my job as Director of Curriculum, Instruction and Assessment. They happened to be previewing books for adoption in the business classes. As I looked at them I asked where the copy of Think and Grow Rich was. She told me she wasn't familiar with it, and I told her it was the biggest selling business book of all time (over 70 million copies worldwide) and they should consider it. A couple of weeks later she informed me the teachers had looked at it and were going to use it the following year. Needless to say I was thrilled. I shared the news with friends. One of them shared the news with the co-founder of Organo Gold, Shane Morand. Mr. Morand is a personal friend of Judy Williamson, the Director of the Napoleon Hill World Learning Center. The next thing I know I'm on the phone with Mr. Morand and Mrs. Williamson. They want to support my Definite Purpose of bringing the principles of Napoleon Hill to my district. As a part of that, I started my certification program with the Foundation. Amazing how the Law of Attraction works!

Learning From Adversity & Defeat

"Every Defeat, Every Disappointment and Every
Adversity Carry Seeds of Equivalent or Greater Benefits"

-Napoleon Hill

Remember when I spoke earlier about my Definite Purpose of teaching the 17 Success Principles in my school district? How the Law of Attraction was working and opportunity came knocking? Well so did Adversity & Defeat. It became so prevalent that a close personal friend told us that she was waiting for the Locusts descend next! Here is how things unfolded.

As I was beginning the self-study portion of my certification work, the political winds of change were blowing in my school district. We had a newly elected Board of Education, which included some members who openly campaigned to get rid of our long time Superintendent. Within a few months the superintendent took a new job. This led to three superintendents in a two year period. During this time of transition the leadership of the teacher's association decided that they also wanted some changes. In my role as Executive Director of Human Resources I dealt with all manner of issues with all employee groups. There were some very difficult decisions that I was in charge of handling that didn't sit too well with the association leadership. This led to a very public year-long campaign to have me removed from my position. The lightning rod being my wife's right to work as a distributor for Organo Gold, and my role in the adoption of Think and Grow Rich and the desire to teach the 17 Success Principles to students and staff. The print and television media is not versed in the principles of Napoleon Hill, and therefore did not use the principle of Accurate Thinking when they sensational-ized the story around the principle of sex transmutation. For most of the community all they needed to hear was the word sex and they were off and running. One of the leaders of the association went so far as to speak publicly at a Board meeting stating there was no room in our dis-trict for Napoleon Hill or his supporters.

While this was happening in my work life, our personal life was also experiencing Adversity in a major way at the same time. Our oldest daughter was injured during a basketball game and ended up in and out of the hospital twice, one being for five days during a two-month pe-riod. During Sydney's time in and out of the hospital, my wife Stephanie began having health issues of her own. First came a bout with Shingle's that the doctor said came from the stress she was under. Soon afterwards she began experiencing abdominal pain. It got so bad that we ended up in the hospital. An MRI revealed a mass in her abdomen. This news was scary under normal circumstances but was amplified for us because Stephanie is a survivor of Breast Cancer. After a couple of fearful days waiting for test results the mass turned out to be an abscess. A relief, but it still required surgery to remedy. As the health issues subsided we were faced with more adversity. In early 2013 Stephanie noticed a police pres-ence of several undercover officers in our neighborhood. Earlier that month a prominent state official was murdered at his home in a hate crime. What we came to learn was that our next-door neighbor was next in line as this officials number two in the same department. The murderer was captured and killed but was found to have a hit list of the next victims, and our neighbor was at the top of the list. Our neighborhood was under 24/7 surveillance and had a substantial police SWAT presence hidden in the neighborhood. Cameras were placed in and around our entire neighborhood. We were advised by law enforcement to have our blinds closed at all times, not to go out until surveying the neighborhood and not to walk our dog. The primary reasons were we lived in a subdivision of patio homes that were nearly identical in color and design. In addition we lived in the corner unit right next door to the corner unit of the protectee. He and I were the same age, both have two daughters, both wives drive black sedans and we both own Golden Retriever dogs. This lasted for several months. To say the least, this in and of itself made it very challenging to live a normal life. After the threat passed we started building a new home in a neighboring town. We were excited about the fresh start. Shortly after construction started we were dealt another blow, my Mother passed away unexpectedly. She named me executor of her will. This caused extremely hard feelings with my siblings and led to a very emotional and difficult six month process of settling her estate. To top our summer off my daughter Sydney's car was struck by lightning and her car was totaled. It fried the transmission and all the electrical systems in the car. The car dealer and the insurance company said it was a first for them. They had never heard of a car being struck by lightning!

One month after my mother passed away my superintendent left and a new one came in. The new superintendent inherited the controversy surrounding me and the adverse publicity the teacher's association leadership was perpetuating. Ultimately she made the decision to side with the association. In December of 2013 I was summarily dismissed from my position. In other words fired! After 27 years working in public education I was 54 years old and unemployed.

Looking back on all of this almost two years later there are a few things I know unequivocally. First, I understand why friends thought locusts would be descending soon! Second, were it not for my training and understanding of the principles of Napoleon Hill, particularly the principles of Definite Major Purpose and Learning from Adversity and Defeat, my family would not have been able to successfully navigate this difficult time in our lives. Third, I will continue my work bringing Napoleon Hill's philosophies and principles to others through workshops, coaching, speaking engagements and other media. Last, while I no longer work in public education my Definite Major Purpose has not changed. I know from my experience as an educator and parent that The 17 Success Principles and the philosophies of Napoleon Hill must be taught to students if they are to be successful in the 21st Century. School districts across the country (including my old district) are struggling with how to teach these skills on top of all the other legislated requirements teachers face already. The answer lies with the philosophies and principles of Dr. Napoleon Hill. Napoleon Hill spent 20 years of his life researching some of the most successful people in the world at the request of Andrew Carnegie, one of the wealthiest and most successful people who ever lived. The result was the publishing of Think and Grow Rich in 1937. Since its original publication it has sold over 70 million copies worldwide and been translated in dozens of languages. Yet his philosophies and principles are not taught anywhere in public education.

Given the ever-expanding achievement and success gap why wouldn't you want students to be taught these principles? Why wouldn't you want them to understand DEFINITENESS OF PURPOSE? The principle Dr. Hill calls the starting point of all achievement and the stumbling point of 97 of 100 people. Why wouldn't you want them to understand the power and benefit of working with a MASTER MIND group? Why wouldn't you want them to understand the benefits gained by GOING THE EXTRA MILE in everything they do, or the power and benefits of APPLIED FAITH? Why wouldn't you want your kids to understand how to develop a PLEASING PERSONALITY, SELF DISCIPLINE and PERSONAL INITIATIVE? Given the information overload bombarding us every hour of every day, why wouldn't you want to understand the principle of ACCURATE THINKING? Why wouldn't you want your kids to understand how to CONTROL their ENTHUSIASM, CONTROL their ATTENTION or learn the benefits of TEAMWORK? Why wouldn't you want your kids to understand the importance of maintaining SOUND HEALTH and how to BUDGET their TIME & MONEY and cultivate their CREATIVE VISION? Why wouldn't you want them to know how to deal with the ADVERSITY AND DEFEAT that they will experience in life, or to understand Universal Laws and how to change their habits as a part of COSMIC HABIT FORCE? Why wouldn't you want them to understand how to go create and maintain a POSITIVE MENTAL ATTITUDE?

I continue to be an advocate for these principles being taught in schools and teach the principles in workshops and other venues. If you are a student, parent, grandparent or anyone interested in the success of our future generation, I want you to consider this a call to action. Ask your teachers, principals and school districts why they aren't or why they wouldn't teach the principles and philosophies of Napoleon Hill.

As the great Mahatma Gandhi said:

"We must become the change we wish to see in the world".

Bio

Chuck DeWayne is an Internationally Certified Trainer for the Napoleon Hill Foundation. He spent 27 years in Education as a Teacher, Coach, Principal, and Central Office Administrator. His Definite Major Purpose is educating children and adults in the Philosophies and Principles of Napoleon Hill. He offers specialized coaching, trainings, classes and speaking to individuals, groups and organizations. He lives in Colorado with his wife Stephanie and two daughters, Sydney and Charlie.

Visit his website at www.chartyourpurpose.com or drop him a line at dewaynenetwork@gmail.com.

How I Became A Rock Star

By: John Westley Clayton

Before my beginning

A FLAME BURNED inside me before I was born; one that could not be extinguished no matter what—and the 'no matter whats' were already lining up around the corner, scrapping with each other in a competition to see which would challenge me first, and which might ultimately defeat me.

And so the stars threw more fuel on my fire to strengthen me. I would be different. I would be victor. And I would champion others. The die was cast—bring it on.

I was thrust into chaos before I saw daylight.

In order to rise from the ashes one must be burned. And so came the classroom of life's lessons I'd repeat until I became an expert at moving on from setbacks. For without that expertise I could not graduate from survival, become a master thriver, and then share life's lessons with others.

The beginning: A Blessing in Disguise

My birth-mother—already a single parent of two when I was conceived—was engaged to my father who, before my birth, died as the result of falling off a cargo ship on which he worked.

Believing she would not be able to raise three children alone, she decided to place me for adoption.

It's hard to look at the tragedy of death as a blessing, but it was. My birthmother's situation required a solution. That solution placed me in another classroom.

A wonderful woman named Berta, who owned a bar in New Orleans, had a reputation of listening to and helping others. She'd wanted a child for a long time; she'd lost one baby at birth and doctors told her she'd never have another.

Believing she'd never have another child—based on the diagnosis of professionals—and wanting a child more than anything else in the world, created a powerful force within Berta.

The two women worked out a handover; absent of legalities and setting me up for a ripple effect of immense proportions.

"You become what you think about."

— EARL NIGHTINGALE

Everyone's thinking not only dictates ones actions, but changes ones chemical makeup. Berta's biology was imbalanced from the earlier death of her infant. Her belief system was reinforced by the words of respected professionals. Berta couldn't become a mother again because she'd stopped *thinking* like a mother.

Once I was *her* son, the chemicals that allowed pregnancy rebalanced.

Eleven months after my arrival she gave birth to a healthy baby boy. Not long after, she divorced, remarried, and had two more children: a boy and a girl.

Meanwhile I prepared for center stage. I experienced the love of a kind woman, the only woman I'd ever think of as my mother. That ember inside me—that knowing there was something out there for me—continued to glow.

At the same time as being nurtured by my mother I was subjected to the outcomes of her choices. The people she involved in her life had a profound influence on me: their actions affected my thinking. If the world was a classroom then everyone was my tutor. And those teachers threw pop quizzes like no one else could, testing my inner strength.

I had to be strong.

"Any idea, plan, or purpose may be placed in the mind
through repetition of thought."

— Napoleon Hill

Rough Childhood

My mother's new husband, Sammy Davis—not the famous one—grew
up on the hard streets of New Orleans with an abusive father. He owned
a bar and diffused trouble daily—which created enemies—which drew
him into more fights.

Sammy had seven children from two previous marriages, and two
more from Berta. Eight to ten children romped through our two-
bedroom home at any given time (and Berta babysat other children).
Competition for attention was fierce, and the status quo for behavior did
not fit the standard I'd set inside myself.

Sammy was abusive to all of us, but had more of a beef with me, but
at the time I was unsure why—I didn't find out about my adoption until
years later after my mother passed away.

Looking back, perhaps Sammy did not consider me a real part of the
family. His dislike may have also had to do with Berta's affection toward
me, since she linked my arrival to the change in her fertility.

Hard times hit when the bars that Sammy and Berta owned were
forced to close.

The way people handle all situations is based on their belief systems
which can be traced back to one thought which has been thought over
and over again to become a belief. Essentially, a habit.

Yes, one thought is extremely powerful when it is thought over and
over again. The million-dollar question is: will that be a positive thought
or a negative thought?

The way Sammy handled hard times was the way he handled all
setbacks: unpleasantly. His thought process was based on violence.

Sammy's example of a father's role was his own father, who—one action at a time—influenced Sammy's belief system. Sammy's life was steeped in negativity at work and at home.

The examples that played out before me were often negative but, each time I witnessed violence or found myself victimized, I connected to an inner energy. One thought: success. No one could beat that out of me. It was a thought that I thought over and over.

> "Against the grain should be a way of life. What's worth the price, is always worth the fight."

> — NICKELBACK
> (Song: *If Today Was Your Last Day*. Album: *Dark Horse)*

The white sheep of the family, I received good grades and never got into trouble. I always looked at my situation with an inner knowledge that I could surpass my poverty-stricken childhood. In essence I suppose it was an affirmation before I knew what an affirmation meant. *I will surpass my poverty-stricken childhood.*

The chaos of family life continued all through my school years. The promise of a part time job and a driving license offered a taste of freedom during my high school years, but for work and wheels I needed a birth certificate and social security card. The solution was that Sammy officially adopted me. In hindsight, I don't know how that was possible—perhaps he knew people?

Many of the situations to which I was exposed threatened to extinguish that fire inside me. But I persevered with directed thought. *I am destined for success.* To keep the flame ignited I knew I had to continue thinking positively. Friends and family looked at me as the one who would break out and become the first millionaire. I had no examples but knew success was out there somewhere and there was a way to get it. I simply needed to find that way.

When I graduated high school as an average Joe I wanted to get away from the abuse. I found full-time employment and moved out.

Out with the old, in with the...old.

I knew that moving out was the best thing I could do to escape. Sadly, my home life combined with the novelty of freedom influenced my decisions, the results of which revealed that I had more growing up to do.

A pattern emerged: party all night; go to work without having slept.

I'd graduated from high school but I had years to go in the school of life—my apprenticeship was just beginning. My order of a slice of freedom came with a side of partying. For a time 'undisciplined attitude' replaced the dream of success. It sat on my affirmations like a lead weight.

Then I met a girl. We married and had a daughter, and though the partying subsided, it didn't end. Even though I acquainted myself with self-help material, immaturity and stupidity (on both sides) caused the marriage to end seven years and another daughter later.

"Even if you fall on your face, you're still moving forward."

— Victor Kiam

Freedom from my growing-up home had come with a price: responsibility. Release from another setback—the end of a relationship—was offset with additional burden.

Out with the old, in with Napoleon Hill

Though I wasn't ready to step on stage, it was time for another script: one which would enhance my role. Enter Napoleon Hill. I immersed myself in his principles. Spark burst into flame and began to blaze. The knowledge inside me clicked with the new information I consumed. Cue the next act.

I knew it would take a lot of work to get from where I was to where I wanted to be, but this time I was prepared. I began to grasp the power of desire.

"The starting point of all achievement is desire."

— NAPOLEON HILL

Oh, and I had that desire. I'd had it before birth, and I'd clung to it when distractions flew in my face. I moved forward. I began to see proof that if someone wants to see change, they must live that change; that, like everyone else, I would not find success with an ineffective mentality.

I devoured every word in *Think and Get Rich*, and dissected every concept. I embraced going the extra mile and celebrated the results it produced for others and for me. I put faith into every step. I practiced reciprocity. Autosuggestion became everything Napoleon Hill professed it would be. I held a vision—an incredible vision. My positive mental attitude almost knocked me over. I learned to channel my persistence. Yes the flame burned within—my mind was on fire.

"Success is going from failure to failure without losing
your enthusiasm"

— WINSTON CHURCHILL.

As is the case with true success, adversity reared its ugly head a number of times. Reinvention, renovation, and restoration were essential for further growth. And because I held true to Hill's philosophy, I moved through and responded instead of reacting. I continued to build myself.

I was based in St. Bernard Parish in Louisiana when Hurricane Katrina roared along the Gulf Coast. The deep sadness I felt for my fellow citizens was overwhelming. My heart ached for my own losses—everything gone.

At the time of the disaster I was visiting in California. Shortly after Katrina's rage I decided to put down roots on the west coast.

Roots – easy to establish when one has nothing left? Or, harder? Either way, attitude is everything. Roots take time to establish; a transplant is more accurate since our attitude knows no geographical boundaries.

I held the principles of persistence and positive thinking and I knew that I was destined for greater things. My inner strength reinforced that belief and Hill's values backed me one hundred percent.

I reviewed. I reset. I looked forward. I looked forward. Oh, did I look forward.

"Start with the end in mind."

—STEPHEN COVEY

And when history repeated itself in the form of the 2008 recession, I did not fall. I was prepared. Frustrating as it was to run through savings when my work in the luxury clothing industry ended, I was able to review, reset, and look forward. In fact I did more than that. With my knowledge from *Think and Grow Rich* the stars aligned perfectly. I held a PhD in life; maturity allowed me to continue to upshift Hill's information.

Cherish your visions and your dreams as they are the children of your soul, the blueprints of your ultimate achievements.

— NAPOLEON HILL

All my life I'd dreamed about the ultimate extension: that after reaching that multi-defined place—success—I'd teach people how to do the same.

Now it was in reach. I'd needed all these things to happen to me. How would I know how to recognize defeat, define it, understand it, and conquer it if I hadn't experienced it?

Every adversity, every failure, every heartache carries
with it the seed of an equal or greater benefit.

— Napoleon Hill

I set about creating a **Definite Major Purpose**; the keystone missing from my life. I wrote a program that explained how to go from the person you are to the Rock Star you want to become. The stars were not only aligned, they danced in the sky and lit my way to the center stage of my life.

And I learned that learning never stops; a good thing, because I never wanted to stop learning.

When I discovered the Napoleon Hill Foundation, which offers courses to become certified as an instructor to teach Hill's principles, the flame inside me flared. I took the courses and received accreditation.

Fired up, ready for anything and everything—and wanting others to share in the same—I took my words, my philosophy, and my experience and created Rock Star 4 life.

"'Cause we all just wanna be big rock stars."

— Nickelback
(Song: *Rock Star.* Album: *All The Right Reasons*)

Rock Star 4 life's methods are delivered via various platforms and cover a multitude of topics including business strategies, personal coaching, sales, health, and relationships.

"Do it right here and now. It means everything"

— Van Halen
(Song: *Right Now.* Album: For Unlawful Carnal Knowledge)

To create a Rock Star in yourself, contact me at info@johnwestley.com or visit my website at www.johnwestley.com.

"For those about to rock, we salute you."

— AC/DC
(Song: *For Those About To Rock*. Album: *Who Needs Who*)

"You are who and what you create yourself to be."

— John Westley Clayton

Bio

Certified Napoleon Hill instructor, John Westley Clayton, motivates individuals, inspires business leaders, and moves mountains.

His personal brand of inspiration, Rock Star 4 life, is delivered from various platforms and presented with candid honesty and a genuine enthusiasm toward everyone's dreams. His active involvement and solution-oriented vision are backed by solid experience in business and sales. His extraordinary life story is worth the backstage pass. Clayton does not simply perform; he is the concert.

Got a dream? John Westley Clayton will put you center stage.

Got a pulse? John Westley Clayton will get you dancing to it.

Got a heartbeat? John Westley Clayton will get you rockin' to it.

Visit his website at www.johnwestley.com or drop him a line at info@ johnwestley.com

CHANGING MY LIFE

By Aristoteles Nielsen

WHEN I WAS about 25 years old, I discovered a life changing philosophy, thanks to my best friend Pablo. The philosophy he introduced me to was **The Success Philosophy of Napoleon Hill.** Reading Hill's classics like "Success through a Positive Mental Attitude", written with W. Clement Stone, "Think and Grow Rich" and "The Law of Success" at a young age, was very important for the formation of my character.

Applying success principles in my own life was a new experience that made me stronger and helped me to have a new and better perspective on my life forever. My purpose in writing this chapter is to share with you my testimony on how I applied the principles of success in one of the toughest moments of my life. I want to tell the world that these principles work for everybody. This practical philosophy of success can be shared in all types of environments, especially where there is need for clarity and support for those of us who suffer losses or need guidance on how to survive life's challenges.

MY DEAR FATHER

It all started when my father's wife called me up after two years of not seeing him, to tell me he had severe cancer in his throat. As my dear dad had no money to pay for decent medical assistance, he was hospitalized for a few days in a state hospital in Buenos Aires, Argentina, where we lived at the time, and where I live now.

After the doctors studied my father's case and made their final diagnosis, they said my father could leave the hospital and get medical attention without being hospitalized. As days passed and the medical attention was lacking in quality and quantity, my best friend Pablo suggested that I take my father over to the United States to get a second medical opinion. Pablo also suggested that I take along with me a copy of **Think and Grow Rich** and a copy of **Success through a Positive Mental Attitude** for support.

At first I resisted my friend's suggestion to travel overseas. I thought there was no need to take my dying father for a second opinion on such a long and costly trip from Argentina to the United States. But my dear friend assured me that this was the best thing I could do for my father and myself. I was then faced with a dilemma: Should I go the extra mile for my father? Was it worth going for a second opinion against all odds? What was the best thing to do in such a painful circumstance? My father's illness was growing rapidly. We had to move quickly and with determination and conviction to determine the right and best thing to do for him. My mother, and other well intended people, advised me not to take him abroad. They thought the best option was to send him home to die in peace. But, once again, my best friend Pablo insisted strongly in creating a scenario of hope for my father. His determination and conviction of what was the right thing to do for my father's situation finally took place in my mind and my heart. I had only one Dad and he possibly had one chance for healing. I needed a strong PMA (Positive Mental Attitude) to move forward.

After I decided to commit to do anything possible to help him, I started my crusade and took him over to the United States immediately. I borrowed the money for the trip and got his passport in a matter of hours. Usually a passport in my country is delivered in no less than 15 days but, my determination and burning desire was so strong that I convinced the Head Officer of the Bureau of Passports to provide me with his passport in less than two hours. I said to this Director "My father's dying and I need his passport now". I will not accept NO for an answer, my father needs his passport... please!" Then, almost immediately, the magic happened. My dad got his passport and a chance for his cure.

Looking back, after reading the story of the girl that demanded that her mamma needs her 50 cents from an unwilling man described in the initial chapter on Desire in Think and Grow Rich, I affirmed *that "Whatever the mind can conceive and believe the mind can achieve"*. The powerful story of that little girl in defense of her mother was my story too, but I was in defense of my father's health and life.

Think and Grow Rich in Times of Sorrow

Once we arrived in America, I had no help from my relatives living there, including my brother and my aunt. Nobody wanted to help my sick dad or myself. The only exception was an old friend of mine that was living in America. This kind person, Peter, literally opened his house to me and my father. Peter called his hospital and got an appointment for my father to have a second medical opinion. A cancer specialist told me that my father could be given a spot in a pilot program at a medical center that specialized in advanced stages of throat cancer. The chances of saving his life were slim, but it was worth a try. After 3 months of struggle, he eventually passed away, despite having world class medical attention at almost no cost.

During those 3 long months with dad, I read Think and Grow Rich at least 5 times. It was very painful to see my father each and every day with almost no improvement. Napoleon Hill was my counsellor in those lonely nights of despair and sadness. My connection with my family back home was through mail or by phone, as the internet did not exist yet in 1990. Of course my American friend Peter and his family were there supporting me. He let me stay at his house during those 3 months. He really went *the extra mile* for me during that period. He also was my support group, and my new mastermind in my crusade for saving my father's life.

As I didn't want to take advantage of my friends generosity, one month before my father died I got a job working with a gardening company; It was a heavy job and I had almost no experience, but I did it in order to have some money to pay gas and part of my living expenses. I also got a second job doing translations from English to Spanish for a political party. So, even though my dear father was dying, life was good to me. My aunt in Hawaii started sending checks to help me.

As days passed, and as my father's life was coming to an end, I felt a very pleasant feeling of inner peace. I was in a state of total faith that I was going to survive the loss of my father. His treatment was not helping his condition. Doctors, nurses, social workers, and priests were all extremely nice to me. Everybody was very friendly and supportive of my situation. I never in my life felt such a feeling of support and warmth as I received from the people I met during that time. They were all part of my mastermind support group. Deep inside of me I knew they gave their best efforts to save my father by Going the Extra Mile and having Applied Faith.

The day he passed away, nobody called me from the hospital. I arrived ten minutes, or less, before he closed his eyes forever. I entered the room and, after a few minutes, he opened his eyes, glanced at me a little, and then closed his intense blue eyes forever. I called the nurse and all of a sudden the priest came in, and prayed aloud. I will never forget those deep words he said on behalf of my father. I could feel how his soul was leaving his body and imagined that his spirit was elevating up into the sky.

A couple of days later my dad was buried. Only my brother and I were at his funeral. He was buried next to his father's, my grandfathers, grave in Los Angeles.

Refusing no for an answer

Back in Argentina, I was late for starting my last year in college. At that time I was studying Human Resources and the Dean of my school rejected my admission, as the semester had already started a few weeks before. I almost lost my year and, again, my best friend Pablo challenged me with the words: "Are you going to accept a "No" from an insensitive

Dean? ". Pablo demanded, "Go to the Chancellor, or the maximum authority of the University, and tell your story". "Use the Napoleon Hill Principles, like you did to help your father".

So I waited outside the Chancellor's office at the university for almost ten hours and I was finally able to speak with him for a few minutes. Against all odds, after he read my detailed letter, he asked me to come into his office and then asked me a few questions. "Is this all true that you have written here? "Indeed Sir, I replied". Immediately the Chancellor called the Dean of my School and ordered him to accept me in the Senior Class so I could finish my college degree.

I still see that Chancellor almost daily. His name is Dr. Fraga and we eat lunch in the same dining room at The University Club of Buenos Aires. He is in his late 70's or early 80's now. He doesn't recall the hand he gave me at that time but I sure do!

The Gift Is in the Giving

After I earned my degree, I started my career as a Human Resources Professional, first working for big companies, and then as an Independent Consultant. During my twenty five years as a professional, I lived through many different circumstances where I applied the Success Philosophy of Napoleon Hill. It wasn't until 2013 where I made the decision to further my study in the success principles by going to a certification class in Ireland, where I met all the wonderful people from The Napoleon Hill Foundation, and earned my certification as a Napoleon Hill Foundation Instructor. That experience changed my life again and, if I have to say why I decided to get the Certification, it is because I wanted to help others to use these positive and noble principles. These principles helped me when I needed them, and now I want to pay forward all the benefits I received from this philosophy.

In order to complete my Certification, I chose as my service project to volunteer helping homeless people in a shelter supported by my church. Since I meet the guests, as we respectfully called them, I work two days a week as a counselor with them. I also teach them The Principles of Success and we play Achievus, the Napoleon Hill table board game invented by my friend and partner Jeremy Rayzor. Discussing success principles with people that are literally homeless is such a privilege to me that it is hard to explain. "The gift is in the giving". When I see those people struggling and fighting to keep ahead in life despite their situation, there is a lesson in it for me. Listening to them talking and discussing the success principles is something that I never dreamed of, and so I want to thank the Napoleon Hill Foundation for supporting me, and advising me, to "do something for others". I literally followed through with that advice and I am receiving a lot in return. I believe that this philosophy is making me richer in many ways that I never thought of before. This philosophy of success has been created "to help the brother". The knowledge and application of these principles on behalf of our fellow men makes us richer every day. It is our choice, in the end, to use it wisely.

So this is the way I have to be able to thank, and return all the benefits received over the years, to the people that helped me in my times of struggle. I want to especially thank my best friend Pablo for teaching me this philosophy, and this chapter is my testimony of gratitude to Peter, and all those that helped me in my time of sorrow.

Bio

Aristoteles Nielsen is a Certified HR Organizational Behavior and Development Consultant with 20 + years' experience in Latin America, working in strategic consulting assignments for multinational firms such as Exxon Mobil, Clorox, P&G, Zurich Insurance, BP, Coca Cola, Ford Motors and many others in Latin America.

In 1994, Aristoteles had established Nielsen Associates Int'l., a Latin America based consulting firm formed by trained professionals in the fields of Management, Psychology and Human Resources; The company focuses their practice in Human Capital Planning, Management Development, Performance Development and Training for Corporate Management and Middle Management positions. He is also a motivational speaker and trainer in 17 Success Principles of Napoleon Hill. See more at www.nielsenasociados.com

Aristoteles Nielsen is also President of the Napoleon Hill institute of Argentina since 2013. He represents Achievus in Argentina, a tabletop famous game based in the principles of Napoleon Hill. He's got his Certification as a Napoleon Hill Leader Certified Instructor also in 2014.

From Desperation to Inspiration

By Sandra Ruiz

When Andrew Carnegie commissioned Napoleon Hill to interview the most successful men of their time, he wanted to prove his hunch that success had a formula. He believed the folks that happened to stumble upon these success principles reaped its great rewards. This premise sparked my curiosity about the success of our 36-year-old family business. Granted it was not a phenomenal success like Apple or Microsoft, companies established around the same time. However, we managed to beat the Small Business Administration's stats on small business survival and created a great livelihood for our family and hundreds of other families throughout almost four decades. I wondered if we happened to stumble upon some of these success principles as well, and if so, which ones? I decided to go back in time and trace our small family businesses' journey. To my surprise, we did indeed unconsciously uncover and embrace the following principles.

Adversity and Defeat

"Every defeat has the seed of equivalent benefit."

Napoleon Hill

Let's begin with the beginning. The end of May of 1979 found us young, carefree and childfree. We had just celebrated our eighth marriage anniversary. The pink rhododendrons were in full bloom decorating the front of our modest split ranch. We were now proud homeowners for two years. My husband had moved up the ranks in his company, a local manufacturer of large copy-stand cameras and was making a very comfortable salary. We felt we had arrived. We were enjoying a great life and looking forward to an even brighter future. Little did we know when the month began that the winds of change were about to knock on our door. Before the month was over, so was our blissful life. My husband's boss informed him that his position as Service Manager was terminated. He didn't deserve to be fired. He greatly enjoyed his work and was completely devoted to it. He liked his boss, the business owner, and was fiercely loyal to him. We were both appreciative of all he had done for us. The news came as a complete shock to us. We couldn't believe it! Sadly for us, the company had outgrown the expertise of the entrepreneur that started it. They brought in the consultants and decided to move the company in a new direction, one that did not include my husband. What were we to do? Where was he to go? Would we have to relocate to work for a competitor? Could he possibly go back to Chemical Engineering?

Six years before, during the turbulent recession of 1973, my husband graduated as a Chemical Engineer from New Mexico State University. We traveled that May from New Mexico to New York, armed with a box full of resumes. We slowly made our way East, like a resume dropping Johnny Appleseed, hoping to plant the seeds of future employment and a future home. We ended up at his brother's apartment in Yonkers, New York, exhausted and disillusioned. We moved in with his brother while my husband frantically searched for a full-time position in his field. To make ends while he continued to search for professional employment, he accepted a job with a small manufacturer of copy stand cameras. The was a temporary income solution. Those were hard times, and steady work was hard to find. Fearing he would be considered overqualified or transient and rejected he made no mention during his job interview of his professional degree. Temporary slowly became permanent and permanent turned into a career in an industry far removed from the world of Chemical Engineering. A career he was now enjoying and thriving in. He made his way up from the production floor to senior management. His aspirations to work as a Chemical Engineer began to take a back seat and slowly disappeared. Now six years later, he felt his window of opportunity to work as a Chemical Engineering had closed long ago. Never working in his chosen field, he did not see that as a viable option. We both felt that sickening feeling of in pending doom that creates a big knot in your stomach. We felt so hopeless and defeated. How could we survive on my meager salary at the health department?

A Definite Purpose

"Study every person you can think of who has achieved
lasting success and you find that each one has had a
definite major purpose."

Napoleon Hill

I still remember clearly my husband, and I sitting at one of the local pizza establishments in Stamford commiserating over our tragic situation. We were feeling both depressed about our future and guilty about spending our limited funds eating out. What a sorry sight we were to behold! A casual observer glancing our way would quickly come to the conclusion that there must have been a death in our family. We were a mess! We made up so many stories! After all, he was now the ripe old age of 35 and over the hill; at least, to re-enter the job force as an entry level Chemical Engineer. And on and on we continued with our sorrowful sonnets of doom and gloom, gloom and doom. Like a slow, and boring Ping-Pong match, we kept bouncing the impossibilities across the booth with little energy and passion. We seriously committed to the pain and the pity of our situation. It was as though we found pleasure in the process of focusing on the roadblocks and obstacles in our way. It did not even occur to us that this could be, in fact, a blessing. We could have easily sat there until closing time drowning in our sorrows. However, the universe intervened. Our pattern of negativity and despair was interrupted by the loud and cheerful voice of our friend Gloria. We looked up. There she stood, like a scolding mother, her hands on her hips and chest puffed up. It reminded me of Wonder Woman, my favorite T.V. heroine at the time. She shouted, indignantly, "How dare you have a pity party and forget to invite me?" We burst into a roar of loud and much-needed laughter and invited her to join us. Gloria masterfully shifted our conversations to ones of gratitude and possibilities. She spoke cheerfully and positive. It was contagious. It wasn't long before we found ourselves infected with her positive mental attitude. And that was the turning point that made all the difference. We now found ourselves sitting at a table cleared of impossibilities. There now was room to a serve a feast of possibilities. And the possibilities started showing up to our surprise, effortlessly. The options became crystal clear and exciting. From our adversity and defeat, there was indeed a "seed of equivalent benefit". My husband would start his own business. For the last six years, he had serviced and visited many of what were known then as "Slide Houses." He met many successful entrepreneurs and observed their operations and business models. He would start his own "Slide House," with the vision of reaching a million dollars of revenue within six years. Our definite major purpose was born!

THE MASTERMIND

> "No mind is complete by itself. All truly great minds
> have been reinforced through contact with others that
> allowed them to grow and expand."

NAPOLEON HILL

Now that we had a definite purpose, we needed to assemble the people, resources and strategy to make it happen. We both agreed I would continue to work and supplement our monthly expenses by drawing on our savings. It was fortunate that we had saved my earnings for the last year and lived off his. Though it was a modest amount, we had a comfortable cushion. At least for the next year, if we budgeted wisely. It hard to believe today, our mortgage was only $500.00! He converted the lower basement level of our small split ranch into a camera room and film-processing lab by purchasing second-hand equipment and improvising as necessary.

Looking back, I can see that once we shifted to a positive mental attitude, it was much easier to co-create it our definite major purpose. We then proceeded to enroll the right people into our mastermind. Our biggest hurdle was securing the funds needed to purchase the $25,000.00 copy stand camera. We solved that challenge by offering his former boss 49% of the startup with a two-year buyout option in return for providing the camera. We also enrolled his advice and expertise to ensure success. He readily accepted the offer. (In two years, we were able to buy him by carefully budgeting our money.)

Because we needed financial advice and moral support, the dynamic duo of our friend Gloria and her husband Mike were the next addition to our Mastermind. They fueled our positive mental attitude with their enthusiasm. Mike, a seasoned CPA for an international operation, gave us the much needed financial advice and how to legally set up the company. We hired another friend, a bookkeeper, to do our books. In the future, there would be others added to our mastermind. Their advice would help us learn new technologies, buy a building instead of renting, and expand our business, but this was the core mastermind during those tender and volatile first years.

The Power of Cosmic Habit Force

"As long as you have the power to form and express your thoughts, you have the power to change the circumstances of your life into whatever you want them to be."

NAPOLEON HILL

I can clearly see how a positive mental attitude and the burning desire to accomplish our definite major purpose activated the power of cosmic habit force. To our surprise, a representative of a local marketing company appeared at our doorstep even before we opened for business! They heard my husband was setting up shop and were anxious to use his services. This agency turned out to be a very lucrative client. And we are very grateful for their faith and support. It helped jumpstart the business within months.

USING APPLIED FAITH: OUR TURNING POINT

"Faith is a state of mind. For it to be useful to you in achievement of lasting success, it must be active not passive faith."

NAPOLEON HILL

The company was now six months old. Our first client, the local marketing company was keeping my husband busy 24/7. Every day, he was up at the crack of dawn and worked many times through the night. Partly due to his learning curve as he boned up on the specialized knowledge needed. Another reason was the nature of the "slide business." It required quick turnaround on projects and last minute changes. Because of the fast turnaround requirement of most jobs were invoiced with an added 100% -200% in rush charges. It was a lucrative business but demanded the working of ungodly hours.

It's in the moments of decision that turning points in your life are created. For my life and our business that day was January 16, 1980. It was my 27th birthday and woke up with an unexpected present, a massive cold! I called in sick with the intention of getting plenty of bed rest and sleep. Unfortunately my attempts to sleep were sabotaged by the constant ringing of the business phone downstairs. I finally decided to come down and see what was happening. I quietly made my way down to the family room of our split ranch; I didn't want to startle or disrupt my husband. As I peered down from the family room door to the basement, I could see my husband at the camera with the phone cradled on his neck frantically trying to shoot slides and answer client questions. I could hear that he was running late on a deadline and was attempting to appease his client. He looked stressed as he continued juggling his one-man show. He shot the piles of reflective artwork stacked up next to him he looked up and saw me. I told I would handle the phone. He nodded with gratitude and quickly proceeded to enter the darkroom to process the film by the hand dip and dunk process he had concocted himself. Less than an hour later, I could hear the handheld blow dryer going as he dried the film. Within minutes, he appeared next to me and proceeded to cut and mount the slides. He looked tired and overwhelmed. The scene elicited many emotions in me. I felt compassion, empathy, sadness, and finally determination. This "one man show" was not sustainable. If it didn't kill him, it would keep him from reaching his major definite purpose. He couldn't keep this up by himself, yet failure was not an option. It was time for massive action. The very next day, I put in my two weeks notice at the Stamford Health Department and joined the fledgling startup. I chose to "burn all our ships" and take the plunge.

This new world of entrepreneurship was exciting and scary at the same time. But with great faith I enthusiastically answered the phones, delivered the work, typed the invoices and eventually made the sales calls. We were now officially a Mom and Pop Shop, committed to the fulfillment of our major definitive purpose, one million in 6 years.

Maintaining Sound Health

"The health of your mind and body cannot be separated."

Napoleon Hill

Four months before I made the decision to jump feet first into our business, I started to cultivate a few new habits that would prove to be of great value to our future success. I began to journal every day and race-walk. Every morning I'd be up at 5:00 am and walk for an hour, and walk again for an hour after work. By the time I joined the business," I was no longer race-walking but consistently running. It invigorated me and grounded me to nature. It was a spiritual experience. I also became addicted to journaling. I called it "talking to myself." The act of journaling created space for self-expression and reflection. It helped me stay in the moment and focus. Every morning, the theme song from the movie Rocky would serve as my bugle call. It inspired me to get up and go without hesitation, no matter how frigid the morning was. I cherished and depended on the refreshment and rejuvenation provided by the "me moments" of jogging and journaling. The extra pounds came off; the muscles tightened, and my confidence soared. Boy, did I look hot!

Budgeting your time and Money

'Tell me how you spend your time and how you spend
your money and I will tell you where and what you will be
in ten years."

— Napoleon Hill

I was now working with my husband for almost a year. We hired our first employee and streamlined the workflow. We started to realize the business vulnerability of depending on one client. We needed to acquire more clients. Remember, we attracted the first one through the power of Cosmic Habit Force. Since we did not understand Cosmic Habit Force or the Law of Attraction, we had no idea how to replicate it. We decided we needed a salesperson. And since we couldn't afford one yet, I'd have to take it on. There was only one little problem; I hated cold calling and rejection! I think it was more than hate. I was allergic to it! But I was committed to our major definite purpose. Remember? Failure, was not an option? So I decided to play a game. And make it a game easy to win, the 9:30 to 11:30 a.m. game. I decided I could endure anything for two hours. I set up a may shift sales hub leveraging the wall phone in the tiny kitchen.

The rules were as follows:

1. Sales call would take place between 9:30 a.m. or after 11:30 a.m. Not a second before or a moment after.
2. Be prepared and ready to go. I would be all dressed with all my collateral, business cards ready to go in the event I was invited over. (In those days, that was a possibility!)
3. Scan through the Stamford Advocate's People in the News section and sent letters of congratulations to corporate folks promoted.
4. Follow up with a phone call after one week.
5. Keep one index card per contact with all phone interactions in my repurposed recipe box. (That was my CRM).
6. Do it every, regardless of how you feel.

Armed with my newly formed rules of engagement; the sales game began!

In the beginning, it was disheartening but it was much easier than today. People answered their phones. However, they either told me they were all set or to try again in a few months. Bottom line: We don't want to hurt your feelings; thank you but no thank you.

Persistence Pays off

> "Persistence is an essential factor in the procedure of transmuting desire into its monetary equivalent."
>
> NAPOLEON HILL

One of my first sales calls was to the Graphics Department Manager for a Fortune 100 company in the neighborhood. I am sure I must have called her over 50 times. I was beginning to lose faith. Our typical conversation went something like this: "Hi Patty, this is Sandra from Slideffects, Inc.

Remember, the slide production house right down the corner? I'm calling to touch base. How are you? I was wondering if you have any pressing little projects we could support? And the answer would consistently be: "Thanks for reaching out, but I'm all set right now." It was discouraging. However, I committed to playing the game. I would visualize driving down Stillwater Road turning onto Long Ridge Road making my way to picking up our first job. Visualizing inspired me to be persistent and follow my self-imposed game rules. Eventually, my persistence was rewarded. I fondly remember that "magic moment." I was on the phone with Patty, again. I had just completed my usual newbie sales rep "touching base" schpiel. I paused and waited, anticipating her usual response. Instead, I heard silence on the other side, a very long silence. And then she said hesitantly, "Well Sandra, I am standing here staring at a box of slides that need duplication. If you can be here within half an hour and pick them up, the job is yours. And because I followed the rules of the game without fail, I was dressed and ready to go! I excitedly responded, "Patty, I will be there in 5 minutes" and I was. We eventually became a vendor of choice for her organization. This woman later became a good friend and mentor. She taught me much about graphic design, typography, and printing. She made amazing zucchini bread that she generously shared with me for decades until she was transferred back to Rochester, NY.

GOING THE EXTRA MILE

"Render more and better service than you are paid for,
and sooner or later you will receive compound interest
from your investment."

NAPOLEON HILL

And finally, the one principle that I attribute above all others for our businesses success and longevity was "going the extra mile". In the beginning, this meant working from early morning to past midnight. Many times, we worked non-stop through the night. Octobers were so hectic; thinking back all I remember is as a blur. I remember one time my parents surprised me with a visit, and I could not take more than 30 minutes to spend with them due to our workflow. My knees and back would hurt from the hours of standing and bending in front of the Photostat camera. We worked 20 hours a day. Those days are now affectionately remembered as the "the dog days of the slide houses" by those of us that sacrificed everything, including sleep to produce those corporate slide presentations before computers or Power Point. One project we worked on very early on almost killed us! It was for a Fortune 50 corporation in Fairfield, CT. Even with the support of two freelance artists, my husband and I worked two days straight without sleep. It was one of those jobs where things kept going wrong and the client kept making last minute changes, but we persisted. We delivered the job together to keep each other awake during the 20-minute drive to Fairfield. We both fell momentarily asleep at the same time while on the Merritt Parkway and almost got into an accident!

In 1984, our company made its first million. One year ahead of our projection! As I look back, I now realize that even though we did know Napoleon Hill's 17 principles of success by name, we stumbled upon and embraced them nevertheless. They are the reason we beat all the odds against small business success and are still standing today, a multi-million dollar enterprise, strong.

These principles included:

- Learning from Adversity and Definite
- Developing a definiteness of purpose
- Establishing a Mastermind Alliance
- Using Applied Faith
- Creating a positive mental attitude
- Maintaining Sound Health
- Budget our time and money

- Using Cosmic Habit Force
- Go the Extra Mile

I can only imagine if we had a conscious awareness of Napoleon Hill's 17 Principles and studiously applied them for the last 36 years, we too could very well have become industry powerhouses like Apple or Microsoft. What could have possibly stopped us?

In 2013, my husband and I parted ways both personally and professionally. As part of our divorce settlement, I signed over my interest in the company to pursue my passion for coaching and training. He is still applying the principles subconsciously, "going the extra mile," day in and day out, keeping the company going and growing. I wish him much success.

Bio

Sandra Ruiz-Desai was the co-founder of the award-winning marketing communications firm, Desai Communications. It was in 1979 as Slideffects, Inc. and headquartered in Stamford Ct. Sandra helped drive Desai Communications from its humble beginnings through four decades of technological disruptions and massive change. Inc. Magazine recognized Desai Communications as one the fastest 500 growing US companies in both 2008, and 2009. Desai has also received vendor distinction by Xerox, PepsiCo, and Diageo. In 2011, Desai Communications moved to Norwalk CT.

Sandra is a member of the Women Presidents Organization and Co-President of the Fairfield County Communications Association. Recognitions and awards include DiversityPlus Magazines, Women of Power in 2009 and the WPO/100 Black Men Women of Color in 2011.

In January of 2013, Sandra sold her controlling interest in Desai Communications after 34 years, and she has moved on to pursue other interests.

Sandra now is the Principal and Chief Inspiration Officer of her consulting firm, Sandra Ruiz Enterprises, LLC. She helps corporate and small businesses team reach their goals through a holistic approach that includes the Inbound Marketing methodology, the Best Year Yet productivity program, and Emotional Freedom Technique (EFT). She also runs "Your Best Life Yet" retreats with her business partner Pat Thomas.

Please contact Sandra at Sandra@SandraRuizEnterprises.com

PMA: All day, Every day

By Dave Doyle

For as long as I can remember, I have had a generally positive outlook on life. Even in my teens and early twenties if people complained about things, or were involved in gossip and drama, I would find myself disconnecting and walking away as much as I knew how. I usually had a 'can do' attitude, expected the best from people, always gave the benefit of a doubt, and didn't understand why some people seemed to be perpetually cranky. If there were a negative way to spin a situation these people would find it. It's actually quite impressive when you pay attention to how much time and effort some people put into negative energy. There really are some masters out there!

I first read the book Think and Grow Rich by Napoleon Hill in 2009 and within its pages I discovered that a Positive Mental Attitude (PMA) is actually a principle for success. That excited me because I knew that I had already been using this success principle for many years. It really got me thinking about using it more often and deliberately, maybe tapping into the idea at higher level and to a fuller potential. At that time I made what I call a 'Core Decision'; a decision that, when made, resonates to the core of your being; in your guts and in your heart first, not just in your mind. And that decision was to live every single day with a PMA - On Purpose.

I want to talk more about what that meant for me but first I would like to discuss more deeply the idea of the Core Decision, because I feel that a Core Decision is really the point at which a person ignites their 'burning desire', as Napoleon Hill calls it, to fuel their Definiteness of Purpose.

We all have made Core Decisions in our lives, and continue to do so, but many people are not even aware when they do, and certainly do not know why it is important to be aware of it. When I made a decision 14 years ago that I would open up a franchise restaurant, and ended up doing it with no resources, no money, and no experience, I did it without having a clue how. That core decision fueled my purpose to open the restaurant, eventually buy out my partners, and open a second location. Looking back, now that I am aware of the success principles, it is clear how it all came together.

An example of another time that I made a core decision, which ignited a burning desire, and fueled a definite purpose, was when I decided to learn to play the guitar at 30 years of age. It's my favorite example because it's so simple and relatable, yet it's just as profound in principle as any other decision I've ever made.

My Dad has played guitar since before I was born. I remember countless sing-a-longs around the campfire and at relative's houses growing up. Music was always a part of our lives. In my teens I really got into listening to music but never playing it. I always remember 'wishing' I could play the guitar but never doing anything about it. I wanted to play for people and be able to join in on the family jams, but I had zero desire to put in the time and effort it would take to get there. Meantime, I have 3 younger siblings who all, at one point or another, found the time and patience to learn to play. Fast forward to Christmas, 2003 when my first born son was 6 months old and my parents, siblings, and their families all came to our house for the holidays. I remember the single moment in time like it was yesterday, and I've learned that with any Core Decision this is almost always the case. One evening, Dad was on the couch playing a song and one of my brothers was playing along. Then my other brother was showing my sister how to play a riff for a song. The two guitars kept changing hands and I was sitting on the floor, my back against the wall and my arms wrapped around my knees. I wasn't singing along, I was just watching. Watching how music brought everyone together and how I felt like I was on the outside. I wasn't of course, but in that moment I sure felt it. And in that very moment, my life changed.

This may sound a little over-dramatic but, when you can recall a moment in time 10 years later and still feel that feeling that brings up a well of emotion inside and brings a tear to your eye, you KNOW that you Know. And what you know is that, in that split-second, you truly made a Core Decision towards a new path in your life. In that moment I decided that I would never sit on the sidelines again while my family was playing music. The next time that my family got together, I would be playing along with them. And in that moment I never made a sound. I never said a word. I just felt hungry and determined and a felt a rush of warm, glowing satisfaction that it would be done.

My family left a few days later and by the end of the week, I bought a used guitar from a friend, taped a recipe card with the chord forms onto the front of the body, and started to learn. It took a long time. It hurt. At times, it truly sucked. But I got better. I rang true chords and built up the calluses on my fingers. I learned a few progressions and never looked back.

I am no virtuoso. I am no crooner. I can strum a song and carry a tune and I have a blast playing music around a campfire. I am proud of myself, and grateful for the experience that this story has taught me. We all have examples of doing this, but this simple story, in my opinion, shows the essence of what making a true Core Decision means. A core decision never comes from the brain. It isn't a logical or mechanical choice of weighing the pros and cons and looking at the ROI, or factoring in time and energy. It comes from the gut, the heart, and the soul. It is deep and meaningful, often only to the person making the decision. It ignites a burning desire, fuels a definite purpose, and is truly life changing for the person that makes it.

This is the type of core decision that I made in September 2009 on a beach in Jamaica as I finished reading a $10 paperback version of Think and Grow Rich; to live every day with a PMA – On Purpose.

So what did that mean? At that time, it meant that I had to train myself to get to the point where in any situation that arose, I would be able to keep a positive outlook and move forward without complaining or blaming, and that's what I did. I believe I had a solid foundation to start from, but even so, I had a long way to go. Six years later, I can now see the transformation. I can also see very clearly where others are on the PMA scale. I have made it a point to associate with like-minded people as much as possible so I am often in the company of other positive people. Even then, we can all get better. Many people who consider themselves as positive thinking individuals will engage in negative energy without even realizing it. Certain ideas or philosophies, which outwardly appear to be positive in nature, are sometimes disguised as positive. An example of this might be when a well-intentioned friend or family member is watching out for your best interests and end up sabotaging your confidence and slow down your progress. They feel as though they know better and are helping you, but what they are exercising is their closed mindedness. A closed mind cannot be accepting or encouraging.

My daily discipline was simply to think more positively. Sounds simple enough, right? The challenge is that an unconditioned mind is easily distracted. Heck, a conditioned mind is easily distracted! So here are some of the activities that I did to train my mind to be more positive. I had affirmations that I read and recited daily. I recorded audio affirmations with inspirational background music that I listened to and recited daily. I revamped my iTunes library and created a playlist that contained only songs with a positive message and listened exclusively to that music for 6 months straight. I only read books and listened to audio trainings that were positive and would help me grow. I talked about positivity more often to family, friends, employees, partners, strangers…everybody. I cut back on watching TV, going from 4-6 shows that I watched regularly every week down to one. I came up with my signature tag line: Be Good. Do Good. Always. I started to greet people with what is now my signature move; the High-5. I decided that when anyone asked me 'how are you today?' or 'how's it going?' I would never reply with the standard 'good, you?' and instead I would always say something like 'Awesome!' or 'Fantastic!' or 'Super!' and when I asked them back: 'You?' I would do so with a smile and I would look them in the eye. I became an advocate for the lowly day of Monday. While everyone else says 'I hate Mondays' I say "I Love Mondays!" and when people say TGIF on Friday, I say TGIM on Monday.

All of these simple activities helped me to focus on the specific purpose of living every day with a PMA and have allowed me to grow into the much more positive human being that I am today. These activities and this PMA lifestyle have given me a bit of a reputation. Some know me as the High-5 Guy and have their hand up ready to go when they see me coming. I am asked on a regular basis, "Are you ever in a bad mood?" or people often comment "You are always in a good mood!" and this kind of reputation feels pretty darn good to carry around. I truly believe that this consistent attitude has brought me favor and opportunities and will continue to do so.

So what is the alternative to living with a PMA? I guess it's living with a NMA. Is there really a grey area in between? I'm not really sure that there is. My experience and perception is that people are either generally positive or generally negative. If you think of someone you know who drains your energy because they always create drama or complain or blame their situation in life on everyone but themselves, then they are probably living with a NMA. I feel that it is a small percentage of people that fit into this category, and I truly believe that almost none of these people will ever change. Could they change? Absolutely, but highly unlikely.

On the other hand, I feel that most people are generally positive but they have not chosen to develop their PMA, so many of them may be at a lower level of PMA where life goes on and things are good, but there isn't any effort or thought into being more positive - on purpose - on a regular basis. This is where the masses are and also where there is the most opportunity for change to happen. Until I read about the actual Principle of PMA, I was a happy-go-lucky kind of guy, but had no reason or desire to be more than that in my attitude. I think that simply by sharing the concrete idea of it, more people will invest more effort on a daily basis to be more positive.

I am sharing with you my personal experience about the principle of PMA. I have been on purpose with it for 6 years and am proud of who I am becoming. I have dubbed myself a PMA Professor and will teach anyone who will listen but I will also continue to practice and learn; there is no resting here. It has become a habit for me to have a PMA and it obviously feels good. So my question is this: If you are reading this now, and this concept has become clearer to you, or if you are now consciously aware of this idea more than you were before, what reason would you have for not wanting to live On Purpose with a PMA from this moment on?

I challenge you to re-read the above question again. And again. Now answer that question.

> "My purpose is to create and instill more positivity in
> this world through my example and the sharing of my
> experiences of living with PMA every day."
>
> — DAVE DOYLE.

I'd like to leave you with 2 Napoleon Hill Inspired poems that I've written.

I read them regularly for inspiration and hope you find value in them too.

Be good. Do good. Always.

WHAT IT TAKES

Think a seed Plant a thought
Deep inside my mind

Water & develop it
And see what you will find
Blooming, drowning
Scorching, growing
Reaching for the sun
Dreaming, fearing
Doubting, musing
Doing till it's done
Conceive, believe, achieve
That's the winner's way
Or destroy, deny, do nothing
And spend the day at play
I'll keep thinking dreams
And dreaming thoughts
And reaching for the sun
And doing all the little things
That get the Big thing done.

PMA

All day and
Every day
In all I do
And all I say
It's a choice
Not a feeling
For Core Decisions
Are never fleeting
PMA every day
Is the only way.

Bio

Dave Doyle grew up wanting to be an entrepreneur. After many attempts in business he opened his first restaurant in 2002 and a second location in 2005. He still owns and operates these as a top performer in the Pita Pit franchise. He has been a top performer since 2009 in his other business as an Independent Consultant with Organo International and is developing a mobile App called Followups to help salespeople be more effective in the field.

Dave has been a student of personal development for almost 20 years. Since studying the 17 Success Principles of Napoleon Hill and taking the Leadership Certification Course through the Napoleon Hill Foundation, he is driven to increase PMA around the world.

Dave's passions are Business and Personal Development but his 'Why' is his family. His wife Amanda and his two sons Ashton and Rhys fuel his passions and bring him home every day.

Connect with Dave at:
LinkedIn: https://ca.linkedin.com/pub/dave-doyle/12/646/987
FB: https://www.facebook.com/quidditycoffee
Periscope: @PMAprofessor

Walking with Faith

By Christy Onabu

"Faith is the connecting link between the conscious
mind of man and the great universal reservoir of the
Infinite Intelligence. It is the garden of the human
mind wherein may be produced all the riches of life."

- Napoleon hill

I feel the only reason I qualify to write this chapter is because I'm per-
severing the good fight of faith. I've decided making success is my only
option. I'm on the journey to success and confidant that I will get there.
I believe my success is already in motion for me to experience all the
twelve riches of life, described by Napoleon Hill.

My Childhood Memories

Born into a polygamous family in Nigeria, my Dad, Thomas Honeycomb
Okochi, had five wives and twenty-two children (one adopted). I was
the seventh child. Growing up was full of challenges. We very rarely ate
three meals a day. My father was in his sixties when I turned twelve; and
you can imagine the energy he needed to provide for his family, leaving
no money for our education. Our family was always behind on paying
school fees, and sometimes, after finishing our exams, the results were
withheld because our fees weren't paid. Amidst all of these challenges,
Dad exhibited wisdom, love, and great leadership. Visitors to our home

couldn't differentiate a mother from her child because he bonded us together so well.

My Mum died when I was two, leaving me during my formative years with my Dad. I'm blessed to have him be my first life mentor. Preserving my father's legacy is my driving force. Motivated as a child in primary school at age nine, I started buying and selling; earning money to assist him provide for our family. This business model was called 'ARTICLE' among the Igbos in South Eastern Nigeria. You needed a table and stool in front of the house to showcase some food stuff. I started with some Christmas cash as a gift from well-wishers. With a piggy-bank for my proceeds; profits after sales were handed to Dad so he could settle his own bills. He and I became a Master Mind Alliance caring for the family.

"Treat failure and defeat as <u>temporary</u>.... For no man is defeated until he admits defeat in his own mind"

-NAPOLEON HILL

Adversity sowed its seed of equivalent benefit. Dad died November 1993 on the day I was to see him with my fiancée with our traditional marriage invitation cards. The wedding was deferred to May 21, 1994 till the period of mourning was over. Much had happened to depress me, yet my inner voice kept saying, *"Dare to be different, dare to dream and work your way to success. Christy, yes, you can keep your Dad's legacy alive."* Having engaged in business and sales since childhood, the desire to always have multiple streams of income became a part of my thinking.

I graduated from the university in 1987 with a B.Sc. Honors in Applied Biochemistry. For two years I remained unemployed, all the while continuing with my small business. I dyed fabrics and bought rice cheap and sold them for a profit. In 1991 I was hired by the Nigerian National Petroleum Corporation and my husband also got a job.

"No man is free until he learns to do his own thinking
and gains the courage to act on his own initiative."

- ANDREW CARNEGIE.

"Personal Initiative is the DYNAMO that pushes the
faculty of imagination into action. It is the quality that
creates a major purpose, as well as all minor purposes."

- NAPOLEON HILL

FINDING MY TRUE SELF

In October 2003, I decided to go into the network marketing industry
and sponsored my sister Florence. A few weeks later, Florence had a
nearly fatal auto accident that kept her incapacitated for months. Both
of us wanted to be free from unhappiness, and release ourselves from
mental slavery. With no knowledge of team building and marketing,
Florence handed me books she purchased weeks before her accident.
They were:'Acres of Diamond', 'Think and Grow Rich', 'The Richest
man in Babylon' and 'As a Man Thinketh' as well as several others.
We read those books, shared the lessons and skills we learned and,
as a result, I became a Manager within one month and she became a
Manager in two months. A level most people only reached in a year or
more.

"There is only one person in the world
who can plan your life...YOU."

- NAPOLEON HILL.

Think and Grow Rich became our manual for success and is still the
book we can't let go of. We have recommended this great book to many

people. We developed a burning desire for our goals and backed them up with plans. We achieved both our short and mid-term goals, ultimately leading us to the accomplishment of our Major Definite Purpose. We have been through adversities, and we have also succeeded beyond our wildest imaginations.

After putting in twelve years (1991 – 2003) on my job, I had no savings to show for it. Our house was still under construction, after eight years, and my sister was indebted to the tune of $50,000. The accident was the adversity that got her thinking, while at home sick and in debt, on how to recover and get her business running to pay her loan. We were Thinking and Growing Rich.

Even with broken bones, my sister was able to acquire a management position for herself. I've come to understand from Napoleon Hill Philosophy of success that I need my mind more than I need my hands and my legs. *"Whatever the mind of man can Conceive and Believe, the mind of man can Achieve".* This is the power of applying the Science of Success Philosophy by Napoleon Hill.

My sister was able to pay off the loan and owned the house, which she later sold for $200,000, so she could start and complete two other houses. My husband and I completed our house and moved into it in 2004. These results served as the eye opener that got us to realize what is possible when walking with faith.

My desire to master Success is unquenchable. After subscribing to the Napoleon Hill Foundation's free Thought For The Day and Weekly Ezine, I took the three courses that are part of The Napoleon Hill Foundation Leader Certification process and passed. Thanks to the Foundation's Servant Leaders for teaching us the most effective wisdom available in the entire universe.

"I like to see a man proud of his country, and I like to
see him so live that his country is proud of him."

– LINCOLN

"We have no trouble in giving feeling to speech when
we believe what we are saying!"

-Napoleon Hill

"Our lives begin to end the day we become silent about
the things that matter."

– Martin Luther King Jr. (Napoleon Hill's Nuggets of
Gold, Monday – January 18, 2010.)

We are on a crusade

I'm on a journey to build a Leadership Development Center for the per-
petuation of Dr. Hill's Success Philosophy in Nigeria. The land in Abuja
has already been purchased. It is in the Federal Capital of Nigeria and
Port Harcourt, in Southern Nigeria. I have chosen my associates wisely.
We are on a crusade to help spread to humanity this great philosophy
that gave us freedom to think and grow rich. We are pursuing this mission through my Leader Certification project, called "PROJECT PMA
NIGERIA". Over three hundred copies of Think and Grow Rich are being distributed free from May – October 2015 so people in Nigeria have
the opportunity to study this life changing book. All we ask in return
from them is to provide us feedback, in writing, on the lessons learned
and how they propose to put them into action.

I founded the Thomas Honeycomb Foundation (THF) with the
support of "Change Advocates"; the education platform formed on the
13th of March 2015, for mind empowerment through Napoleon Hill's
Philosophy. I call it our "Mind School". We have successfully held our
quarterly seminars since 2010 and unemployed youths are creating businesses, and becoming employers with employees. Family and work relationships are greatly improving for many of our participants.

The Foundation, with Zakaria initiated "Charity MasterMind" currently supporting four camps of the Internally Displaced People from North

Eastern Nigeria due to the insurgency. Over $25,000 and household items have been donated. THF will partner with these IDP camps and share the success philosophy. Dr. Hill's lessons from adversity and defeat will bring life enduring hope and success their way. Those dry bones will live again!

By September 2015, my foundation will hand over six classroom blocks to the Odiguete community in Edo, Southern Nigeria. So far, $38,000 has already been spent on construction. 3,000 writing materials and bags were donated by Napoleon Hill Leader Certification French Lick Indiana Class and THF. Some of the materials will also go to the improvised schools within the IDP camps. Scholarships are ongoing for unprivileged children from primary to university level.

> "Many millions of people believe themselves to possess wisdom. Many of these do possess wisdom in elementary stages, but no man may possess real wisdom without the aid of the power known as a Master Mind and such a mind cannot be created except through the principle of blending, in harmony of two or more minds. Upon this principle, whether consciously or unconsciously, is founded all the great industrial and commercial successes that are so abundant in this age".

> – NAPOLEON HILL, THE LAW OF SUCCESS PAGE 361).

I'M A TESTIMONY

Currently Six members of the mastermind are taking the "Your Right to Be Rich" home study course and Distance Learning PMA course, all expenses paid by the Foundation. It's important to note here that this was the goal I set while at French Lick Indiana in March 2015. I believe in Definiteness of Purpose, without which success is unachievable.

I am a testimony of the benefit of adversity and applied faith. I have faced many adversities, and never considered them as defeat, rather as stepping-stones to greatness. I am grateful to my sister Florence, Dr. Napoleon

Hill, and all the wonderful individuals associated with The Napoleon Hill Foundation. Special thanks go to my husband, Emmanuel, I call him the Best Man, for letting me Think and Grow Rich, and our son and my nieces; Toby, Adaugo and Favor for bringing out the entrepreneurial spirit in me. To those I give my labor of love and blessings; you are very special to me. You are all the reason I am so happy and looking forward to greatness. You were the force that got my husband and me from zero savings to our current net worth of over $1,000,000 with PEACE OF MIND and respect for all people.

We own cash flow properties now, as part of the attainment of our Major Aim – to 'Build a Leadership Center' that will partner with The Napoleon Hill Foundation and teach our mentors Success Principles to help turn out great leaders that will take my country, Nigeria, to a level of success available to, and beneficial for everyone. I had faith and I applied it – put it into action - and the great reservoir of Infinite Intelligence is supplying abundant resources to me and people around me.

"Whoever you may be, whatever you may now be doing, the PMA Science of Success philosophy will give you a better understanding of yourself and other people so that you may negotiate with others in that friendly spirit which inspires others to cooperate with you at all times."

- NAPOLEON HILL

"Success isn't something you can buy in the big economy package at your local supermarket. It isn't a magic potion you can drink from a silver cup. Every man and woman who has attained any measure of success has done so through work and determination. It isn't enough to say, I'm going to be a success, for success comes only to those who know what they want, who are willing to work for it, and who follow – through regardless of real or imaginary obstacles".

NAPOLEON HILL

IF IT IS TO BE IT IS UP TO ME

— The Napoleon Hill Foundation.

It is also up to you to join our Great Achievers league and become successful and help others become successful. Walk with faith, discover your true self, and succeed. You and I are the ones responsible for making our world a better place.
Christy Onabu
Nigeria.

Bio

Christy Onabu is one of the foremost Nigerian ambassador and crusader of Think and Grow Rich and the Napoleon Hill 17 Success Principles. A coach, mentor and change advocator.

Deputy Manager Distribution with the Nigerian National Petroleum Corporation and Founder of Thomas Honeycomb Foundation, an NGO that is engaged in empowering individuals and groups to find a better way to live and have their dreams accomplished. Initiator, "The Change Advocates" (a mind school) aimed at helping citizens in her country to develop positive mental attitude with focus on Napoleon Hill's principles she considers key to their success. She discovered Napoleon Hill's Think and Grow Rich in 2003 and is currently NHF Certified Leader working on her "Project PMA Nigeria", documenting feedback from over 300 free copies of Think and Grow Rich given out. She holds a Masters Degree in Biochemistry. For more information contact her via email at thcwisdom@yahoo. co.uk;

Facebook: ProjectPMANigeria;

Awaken Your Mind

By Samuel Standley

I BELIEVE THAT the book "Think and Grow Rich" by Napoleon Hill is God inspired. I, and many others, believe that it is only second to the Holy Bible in terms of wisdom and truth about personal success. Napoleon Hill gave to humanity the "holy grail for success" and I am certain there isn't any other book on earth like it.

Hill's work provides fundamentals, basics and cornerstone principles of success. "Think and Grow Rich" is the foundation for many other book on success. As an author, speaker, and a voracious reader, I must confess that I have found no other book like it in the world. Since its publication in 1937, the book is still fresh for today's readers and myself. Life seems to leap out of the pages every time I read it. I was privileged to inherit my grandfather's treasure, a 1937 hardback print of Think And Grow Rich, which he read back in 1975. I am grateful to share with you my "Napoleon Hill Inspired Story".

My Early Academic Struggles

I struggled with school when I was a young boy because of the poor negative village environment in Nigeria that I was raised in. Villagers talked with no discretion, screamed aloud and verbally abused people for every little error they made. Being the first son of my parents, out of nine siblings, you were expected to equal and improve your family position. That killed me mentally and emotionally. I literally died inside, which affected every area of my life. I became an introverted person, and was dejected, with no hope for the future. I was often criticized for things I attempted doing, without any appreciation expressed for my efforts. Fear became my lord and king because I could not IMAGINE a good life for myself. I retreated into my SHELL.

I failed throughout primary and secondary school. Because of my mother's concern for my well being, she kept telling me, "Awaken your mind, awaken your mind, awaken your mind," it seemed like over a million times. I hated having friends and talking to people in my village, and inspiring books became my best friends. I was able to see into the author's positive mindset with my mind's eye. I also read a lot of adventure series books by Enid Blyton including "Secret Seven" and "The Famous Five". I just had to look for a way to resurrect my slumbering mind by any means.

Life Must Go On

Jessica Standley, my older sister, and I sold eggs, iced water, soft drinks, and pot sponges, to name a few. We sold for our mother, with the trays on our heads, in the markets and streets of Port Harcourt, in Nigeria, in the 1970s. Our parents had divorced and, without any substantial money from my father to help, my mother's salary was not adequate. She was employed as an Office Cleaner with the Port Harcourt Local Government Council. She worked hard to pay for our school fees, the house rent and food to sustain our family. Mother didn't attend secondary school. She only had a primary school education. Her father was poor, but she had a brilliant mindset, partly from reading her Bible and daily devotionals. We were really struggling financially but the petty trading still continued.

Surprisingly, the landlord evicted our family from our house in 1979. Why? I do not know. We had to move into an uncompleted building. It was still under construction, had no electricity, no doors, and no windows. *Home sweet home!* We moved in and created a *do-it-yourself* door and windows with mother's wrappers. We could not sleep most nights because we feared intruders. That was until we had enough money to install makeshift doors and windows. After 4 years, another eviction no-tice came and mother wasted no time in getting a plank house for her family, by a muddy riverside. *Life must go on!*

Mother's Secret Words of Success

One morning, when I was 12 years old, my mother woke me up to talk with me about life, and the struggles of becoming an asset to the soci-ety we lived in. I still remember the feeling like it was yesterday. I did not have a magnetic memory, and cannot recall many things I heard or was told at that age. I do remember some things she said because there are some moments in time that just won't leave your memory. This is especially true when your mother awakens you in the early hours of the morning to listen to her inspiring words that would shape your destiny.

Mother had been practicing some success principles, which I never knew before. I found this out in 2003 when she died as I was going through her few books and I saw a book titled, "Think and Grow Rich" by Napoleon Hill (Original 1937 hardback print). To my surprise, I saw my paternal grandfather's name written on the flip side of the cover. Below his name was written *"August 1975,"* the date he bought and read the book. I could now understand why grandpa was a successful busi-nessman. How mother got my paternal grandpa's book I do not know.

My Mind Awakening

I bought and read "Think and Grow Rich" in 1997. I still have my copy, though the pages are falling off from repeated reading. It is said that, *"Repetition is the mother of all learning"* so I read it over and over again. After finding my grandfather's copy, that my mother had been read-ing, it stirred in me the hunger, a real need, to study what grandpa and mother knew that I didn't know. I discovered mother's success se-cret was Napoleon Hill's success principles including DESIRE, FAITH,

PERSISTENCE, and 14 others. She could get whatever she wanted if she pursued it. She was a true workaholic and used to amaze me as a boy.

Mother only had a primary school education, but before she died of breast cancer in 2003, at the age of 57, she:

- Had moved from the position of 'Office Cleaner' and became 'Senior Market Superintendent' as a Civil Servant working under the Local Government.
- Built a 5 bedroom apartment in our home town.
- Had two separate houses in Port Harcourt and Yenagoa.
- Driven four types of cars – Volkswagen Passat, Peugeot 504 and 505 and Mercedes Benz car
- Had about $10,000.00 in her bank account when she died in 2003

Her secret was "Think and Grow Rich," and it worked for her despite only having a primary school education. Mother was not highly educated academically, but she was educated with Hill's success principles. She kept telling her children to "Have an awakened mind", and for this I am grateful. Napoleon Hill tells us *"Whatever the Mind Can Conceive and Believe, It Can Achieve."* She proved to herself that Napoleon Hill's philosophy can awaken a mind when the principles are applied. Mother was my first life mentor and hero, she taught me the mystery about life. I miss her dearly.

As I stood in front of that bookshelf in the bookstore in 1997, one book caught my gaze, "Think and Grow Rich." It was like a bulb turned on in my brain. My mother had always told me about awakening the mind, so "Think" on the book had me wondering even before the "Grow Rich". I was inquisitive, so I bought the book. I was suddenly awakened as I was flipping through the table of content and reading topics like: Desire, Imagination, The Brain, How to Outwit the Six Ghosts of Fear, and others. I realized these are the most important areas I needed to improve in my life. I wasted no time and consumed the wisdom the book contained.

A Village Boy Who Once Embraced Failure

"Man's only limitation, within reason, lies in his development and use of his imagination.... ideas are the product of the imagination."

- Napoleon Hill

It took me a few years of working and stimulating my Imagination and knowing the difference between *Synthetic* and *Creative Imagination* through the guidance of Dr. Hill. In 2001, I authored my first book, "Secrets of the Anointed Word." I also published a second book, "PASS - Pursuing Academic Success & Self-Actualization." Currently I am adding finishing touches to my third book to be published before the end of 2015. I already have scripts of ten other book titles and outlined topics put together. There is no stopping me. My faith is already in motion like a rocket heading for the distant planet Pluto.

All this happened because I had the "DESIRE" to change my life; moved by "FAITH;" saw myself succeeding through "AUTO-SUGGESTION" got some "SPECIALISED KNOWLEDGE;" used my "IMAGINATION;" and through "ORGANISED PLANNING;" made the "DECISION" never to procrastinate again; "PERSISTENCE" kept me focused. The "POWER OF THE MASTER MIND" is in motion with Christy Onabu, my wife Inara Blessing, my mother Stella George and other positive individuals. They are responsible for making my life a motivating one. We are on a mission together to stimulate the minds of youth, adults and elderly people. In the words of Napoleon Hill, *"Truly, 'Thoughts Are Things,' and powerful things at that, when they are mixed with Definiteness of Purpose, Persistence, and A Burning Desire for their translation into riches and other material objects."* Anyone can succeed who applies Dr. Hill's philosophy.

IF MY MOTHER SUCCEEDED WITH ONLY A PRIMARY
SCHOOL EDUCATION FOLLOWING DR. HILL'S
PHILOSOPHY, AND I MADE IT OUT OF ACADEMIC
ADVERSITY, ANY HUMAN WHO CAN READ CAN ALSO
SUCCEED. GUARANTEED!

I am a product of books that I have read, especially, Think and Grow
Rich, which has made me a better **thinker** today. I tell people the same
things my mother told me, "Awaken your mind." Because of the connection with Infinite Intelligence, I have both a Bachelor and a Masters
degree in Education Administration. Who would ever imagine a village
boy who once embraced failure would be inspiring people today?

My Driving Force

As a speaker, I have spoken to thousands of people in my preaching
engagements in Nigeria and the United States. I lived in Lafayette,
Louisiana, USA for six years; working with a Rehabilitation Centre/
Halfway House. I had a weekly class on Mondays tagged; "Live Your
Dreams". My clients included prostitutes, drug addicts, homeless adults
and teenagers. These individuals were in hopeless situations, but we
helped them to understand that they could change their own life. Some
of them had never even heard of Napoleon Hill or his books before. I
had my grandfather's "Think and Grow Rich" book with me in which
I drew lessons from teaching my clients the principles of success. I encouraged them to purchase their own copy of Think and Grow Rich,
so some went to Barnes & Noble, Book-A-Million and even Wal-Mart to
look for cheaper copies.

Lives were truly transformed. Prostitutes found purpose, and hun-
gered to be successful, as they registered for GED programs and even
got accepted into the University of Louisiana, graduated, and are now

social workers helping other people in the community get their lives back together. One of the ladies, ten years older than I, had a man propose marriage to her, and I had the privilege to be the man who gave her hand in marriage to her husband. We still communicate through emails and Facebook. Drug addicts changed their thought patterns and became sober, and went back to enroll in programs that would give them the edge in life. One guy met a beautiful lady, a university graduate, and married her; I attended the wedding. I cannot say "Thank you!" enough for Napoleon Hill's success philosophy. It is inspiring to know that his work is out there in the world, helping people to find meaning for their life.

In the words of Napoleon Hill, *"I believe in the power of **DESIRE** backed by **FAITH**, because I have seen this power lift men from lowly beginnings to places of power and wealth. I have seen it rob the grave of its victims. I have seen it serve as a medium by which men succeeded after having been defeated in a hundred different ways. I have seen it provide my own son (Blair) with a normal, happy, successful life, despite nature's having sent him into the world without ears."*

"Think And Grow Rich" is my second Bible. I do tell Christians in our Church to use it as a companion to the Bible to achieve success; and I quote from it while teaching our Tuesday's Bible Class and Sunday's worship service because the principles of Napoleon Hill are scripturally biblical. Yes they are!

In the chapter on **Desire**, Napoleon Hill said, *"Christianity is the greatest potential power in the world today, because its founder was an intense dreamer who had the vision and the IMAGINATION to see realities in their mental and spiritual form before they had been transmuted into physical form."* (Quoting from my grandpa's 1937 original copy). Igniting desire, taking the initiative and using my imagination was a huge problem to me, but now it's easy for me.

In the chapter on **Faith**, Napoleon Hill said, *"If you wish evidence of the power of FAITH, study the achievements of men and women who have employed it. At the head of the list comes the Nazarene. Christianity is the greatest single force which influences the mind of men. The basis of Christianity is FAITH.... The* *sum and the substance of the teachings and the achievements of Christ which may have been interpreted as "miracles," were nothing more nor less than FAITH.... The classical example of the miraculous possibilities of Faith is to be found in the life of Jesus.... His message changed the world.... and His message reechoed down the centuries.... His message is a challenge to Humanity nearly two thousand years after His death."* (Quoting from my grandpa's 1937 original copy). That is why I teach Hill's principles in Church. I believe Jesus in His days taught men how to "Think and Grow Rich." That's what "Repentance" means, CHANGE YOUR OLD THOUGHT PATTERN OF THINKING AND ADOPT A NEW THOUGHT PATTERN TO "THINK AND GROW RICH."

I truly recommend Napoleon Hill's "Think And Grow Rich" to Christians who aspire to be wealthy in this life.

Napoleon Hill has penned the timeless wisdom of the ancient, for modern day man to apply and become successful. Napoleon Hill is dead long ago, but his work still re-echoes in the minds and hearts of people because his principles are universal and eternal.

Now, I'm determined to be a preacher of the Napoleon Hill's principles of success by organizing seminars for people who are tired of living a low life and hungry for a higher life of success. People need to be taught PRINCIPLES because they are eternal and do not change. Success has no short cut, it is principle oriented, and MUST be applied to succeed.

The two greatest book compilations I have ever read in my life are:

1. The Holy Bible.
2. Think And Grow Rich.

The Bible impacted me SPIRITUALLY, while Think And Grow Rich impacted me MENTALLY.

Napoleon Hill, THANKS!

I encourage everyone who thinks life is useless for them, there's ALWAYS an ANSWER to every CHALLENGE you are going through.

NEVER GIVE UP! GOD HAS SOLUTIONS. I CAN HELP YOU GET THOSE SOLUTIONS!

Bio

Samuel Standley was born in Lagos, Nigeria. He was primarily raised from a humble beginning by his hardworking mother who only had a primary school education. She taught him the basic principles of life while he was a little boy which enabled him to develop a Positive Mental Attitude about life in adulthood, not minding the series of failures he had been through. Controlling his attention was his biggest obstacle.

Now a Pastor, Author, Speaker, Philanthropist and Entrepreneur. With a Masters Degree in Education Administration, he was Provost of Power Bible College and Superintendent of Word Power Chapel, all in Port Harcourt, Nigeria. He worked with Acadiana Outreach Centre Inc. A Rehabilitation Centre in Lafayette, Louisiana as a spiritual counselor where he contributed in changing the lives of many "hopeless" people for them to realise the dignity of life.

He is CEO, **SuccessMind Awakening.** He also oversees Believers Wisdom World Church Inc. aka **The Wisdom City** based in Yenagoa, Nigeria, where he lives with his wife, Inara Blessing Standley and their four daughters: Nyanate, Soteria, Charisma and Agape.

To contact him:
Email - samkstandley@gmail.com
Phone - +2348132858175
Facebook - Samuel Standley

Without a Compass

By Michelle Casey

"The starting point of all great achievement begins with
having a definite major purpose."

Napoleon Hill

We all need a definite major purpose, and my story is almost stereo-typical of what happens to a young woman in western civilization who wanders into obscurity and becomes lost due to the distractions of life.

I was 50 years old when I finally reached for the deeper knowledge and understanding of Think and Grow Rich. As a result, I enrolled in The Napoleon Hill Foundation Leadership courses and became a Certified Leader. Through this amazing experience I was able to identify my definite major purpose in life and begin my journey to the Promised Land.

My Definite Major Purpose: To become a well sought after and highly paid global professional speaker, building a financial legacy to help others reach their individual goals. My dream is to continually propagate the world with seeds of inspiration, love, hope, and peace, leading to great positive effects on this and future generations.

Sounds like a big dream doesn't it? That's what I thought until I studied Napoleon Hill's lessons.

"What the mind can conceive, and believe,
it will achieve."

NAPOLEON HILL

I had been thinking about this idea for several years. It took me quite some time to identify what my message was or how it would be best delivered. I wondered if I should write a book, or two, or even a series. I realized, through my personal life experiences, as well as my 26 years as a hairdresser that I have much to share.

For a long time, I pondered who would even be interested enough to listen to what I had to say, and if it would be relatable or helpful. I questioned if I was even qualified to help others.

I began processing this more fully, after going through many life changes and traumatizing events. I found that life was happening faster than I could write.

In hindsight, I can see that my adversities were simply labor pains for a new life.

My healing journey ensued through many courses and support groups that dealt with my traumas. Surprisingly, I found that through connection with others, I was being identified as a gifted orator. At first, I thought that they were just being nice, but something deep inside of me was calling, and connecting with the words that they said. It was truly an enlightening and inspiring gift to hear this. People approached me, some of whom were complete strangers, encouraging me to pursue public speaking. Speaking became highlighted in my mind as possible platform for my message.

I asked for input from close friends and confidants, including my family. I was so amazed that they not only agreed, but that they seemed surprised that it had taken me so long to make this self-discovery. I concluded that being a speaker might be a better focus than writing. The gifts from natural connections became more apparent and paved the way forward. I decided that writing books would have to come later, noting the difficulty in finding time to write. Besides, I felt I might face more obstacles in attempts to be published, or at least I thought so at the time. It's amazing how the universe brings synchronized opportunities, once you set your course of ACTION!!

It was over 30 years ago, when I was at the tender age of 19 and I took a leap of faith. I left behind my home town in Nottingham, England venturing across the "Big Pond" to America. I'd paused my idea of becoming a history teacher in England, and instead decided to try my luck at living the "American Dream."

Upon arrival, I almost instantly fell in love with the lifestyle and coastal living on the shores of South Carolina, and it's been my home ever since. It's been 32 years since I made that first leap, and I've never regretted it; despite getting lost in a few of life's detours.

My first job in America was working in a beachside arcade as a monitor, which I'd landed due to an opening in my cousin's family business. After a short time, I began shifting between bartending and waitressing jobs working in local seafood restaurants. Needless to say, my circle of friends was limited to young party loving people who lived in the moment, trading their few distant daydreams of the future, for the pleasures of the "here and now". For us, the future was an elusive, timeless idea that needed no attention. I was seduced by tropical suntan oils, the beautiful blue ocean and gorgeous beach bodied boys. Oh boy!

Infatuated by it all, I fell in love and ultimately married too quickly, while in a frenzied state of passion, tightly gripped to a powerful need to *feel* loved. I had only known him for one short and very stormy year, yet still, I wanted to be his bride. I gave my heart away so easily and foolishly. Too soon I found my heart crushed and devastated. Then, to my surprise, toward the end of this very brief marriage, I discovered a tiny little new heart beating inside of me.

Facing down divorce, and the prospect of being a single mother at the age of 24, was both a humiliating and daunting reality that I humbly accepted. I felt that my stupidity and low self-esteem had sealed my fate, as well as affecting the life of my innocent little baby boy. My poor choices conveyed bad judgment, which I saw reflected in the eyes of others, adding to my self- deception and belief that I was an unworthy character.

I lived with guilt and shame for years for being so reckless. I felt that there were so many people in the world, who were much more worthy and had been given so much less to work with. Even though my parents divorced when I was sixteen, I had still come from a good home.

I had no excuse. How could I have squandered my opportunity?

I sought redemption within myself by serving others. My thinking ultimately created an open invitation, by me, to become a doormat that others could step on.

I eventually found grace in a local church, and believed that serving in God's house would bring me closer to God's plan. In many ways, it did. I believed that I had found a second chance, followed by a second husband, and also certain joy, with a second child. Ten years of marriage would pass before I was brought a second helping of new devastation. This time around I learned about the horrors of mental illness and the stigma it carries. I found fear, betrayal, and desperation. All this, while praying that my two children would be spared from witnessing the confusion and anguish of it all. Unfortunately, their teenage years revealed that they were not.

Early in 1990, prior to my second wave of disasters, a life-line from the heavens was thrown to me. It was a chance meeting with a beauty school owner who revived an earlier interest for me with the salon industry. This would open the door that inevitably led me to becoming a hairdresser at the age of 25. Once licensed, I began building my career and clientele in Myrtle Beach, South Carolina. Miraculously, after only 3 years in the business, I opened my first salon, not too long after my second child arrived. I juggled being a wife and a mother while constantly seeking to improve my skills as a hair care service provider. I literally came head to head with my passion every day. I latched onto that line for dear life, and have continued to do so for almost 26 years. I have been so blessed and thank God for it every day.

I have been so grateful for the lessons I've learned and the opportunities I have been given. My hunger for learning continued to fuel my desire for more education, not only in my own field, but in other life areas as well. I yearned to understand the heartache of mental illness and learned a lot through courses in N.A.M.I (National Alliance for Mental Illness). I eventually became a family class facilitator, offering support and teaching coping skills for families caring for an adult living with a mental illness. The need for education and understanding began to overflow in every area of my life. With this in mind, I expanded my communication skills by becoming a Certified Life Coach.

Over the years, I've come to understand how to harness the power of reflective communication. I have applied this in the salon environment, empowering both client and hairstylist relationships, with a particular focus on client consultation techniques. I recognized that many clients and stylists need to develop consistent systematic and effective consultation dialogues, allowing freedom of expression for thoughts and ideas, without the threat of frequent misinterpretations. These systems have been developed in my salon and are shared with clients as well as other salon professionals. With the successes in my own salon and consulting business, I became committed to deliver these proven techniques to the salon industry and beyond. The benefits of these principles are huge in all aspects of personal and business communications.

It was November 2014 when I finally took some time and read Think and Grow Rich, during the Thanksgiving holiday. I'd had the book in my personal library for years and never read it. I dismissed it foolishly, believing it was just about making money. My goal was to be about service only. As a result, my bank statements reflected my philosophy. This was just another example of my lost thinking from my younger days.

After reading Think and Grow Rich, I started to lay out my specific plan and made the decision to make 2015 a "Year of Massive Action." I signed up for the Napoleon Hill Your Right to be Rich Home Study Course and started the study immediately as well as the PMA Online Distance Learning Course. I drove to French Lick Indiana to take the Leadership Course in March 2015. I joined Toastmasters and the National Speakers Association and hired a writing coach. I have become an author and a speaker. My path is clear to me now.

I knew the journey would be a financial commitment and require endless hours of work and dedication, especially at first, but I was prepared to invest the time and money necessary to achieve it. I still give up sleep and special time with loved ones to study, but it has been well worth it. There will be greater benefits through the practice of self-discipline and delayed gratification. I have applied faith and maintained a positive mental attitude, believing and trusting that my health and finances are protected while my purpose on this earth is being fulfilled. Daily focus has deepened this thought process in my subconscious mind, which is connected to infinite intelligence.

I did not realize that these teachings would lead me to the greatest leap in character development that I have ever experienced. It is a complete guide to success in mind, body, and spirit, as well as understanding the balance of service with financial and unlimited prosperity. How does one identify ones definite major purpose? I would say to move in a direction that feels right, and create a path with a strategy and goals. Practice the 17 principles of achievement in every area of your life and review these areas daily. Be mindful in all of these things.

My daily life has more meaning, and a stronger foundation of inspiration, while expanding the possibility for other people's happiness on a broader scale, as compared to just one hair client at a time. I am well on my way to fulfilling my dream of helping others globally.

I believe definite purpose in life is a living thing. I believe it is both spiritual and cosmic before it manifests in the physical world. I believe that we and our definite purpose evolve and grow together. The inception of a definite purpose begins when one starts to recognize the possibility for more than just the "status quo". We encounter a challenge for change, and then rise-up to meet it. It is our choice. The path may not be clear at first, but burning desire will cling to an idea for change, and it eventually becomes both the compass and fuel simultaneously. Even if you're low on fuel, never give up!

Bio

Michelle was born and raised in England and immigrated to America in 1983. In 1997, she became a proud American citizen, after being awarded citizenship in 1997. Her career started in the salon industry as a young hairstylist, advancing as a salon owner and National Educator for John Paul Mitchell Systems. Michelle was also fortunate enough to be introduced to N.A.M.I (National Alliance for Mental Illness), leading her to volunteer in their family support program. Michelle is also a Certified Professional Life Coach offering workshops and seminars in various other fields. In 2015, she became a Certified Leader for the Napoleon Hill Foundation.

Michelle enjoys being an active member in the National Speakers Association and Toastmasters International. Public speaking and education is her passion, leading to the full time development of HairCology ™, which establishes the link between the psychology of hair styling and hair trauma prevention. For more details on my new book go to www.YourHairyGodmother.com and www.HairCology101.com

A Positive Mental Attitude through Adversity

By Shannon McVagh-Janz

Good day - It's a great day for events & coffee! – Is what you will hear when you call my voicemail message! I say it with a smile in my voice and have had numerous people call my voicemail just to hear the message, as it puts a smile on their face.

When I took my first job out of high school, at a tourism marketing association, a fellow colleague, Ronda advised me to always answer the phone with a smile in my voice. She said people can feel your compassion, helpfulness, and genuine care through the phone. Even if the day I was having wasn't going so well, this was something that has stuck with me for over 25 years. I believe the principle of having a positive mental attitude (PMA) started when I was young.

I was attracted to reading books that help you to better yourself. When you read personal development books, you're introduced to things that other people are experiencing, and you find out how to overcome the obstacles, or work towards improving your life. You will often find me in thrift stores, in the book section, looking for different gems that others have given away, as I find tremendous lessons in their stories.

Now as you read the chapters in this book I look forward to someone's story resonating with you and helping you to rebuild or grow in this amazing life we have to live. Every sunrise gives us the opportunity to make a difference in the life of someone else and our own.

My first year in college, at the age of nineteen, was when I was first introduced to the book Think and Grow Rich by Napoleon Hill. It was not however until I was in my late 20's that I began to study the book. Over the years I looked for other family members who enjoyed reading

162

personal development books and came up short in my search except for one person, my Aunt Barb. This I believe was the start to finding like-minded individuals in my quest.

I am the mother of two young boys who are both active in many different things and I am married to a wonderful supportive man. One thing we do all have in common is we enjoy playing hockey. My father was self-employed, and I could see the struggles it entailed, yet I was fascinated with self-employment and what it involved.

In the late 1990's I returned from a year of travel in Australia and I decided to start a new venture in a northern Alberta community, where I only knew one person. I was scared but I didn't let fear hold me back. I wanted to be independent and set my own schedule and so I left to start an event management business.

I specialized in organizing consumer tradeshows and loved building the relationships with the exhibitors over the years. Over a 17 year period I had expanded my network tremendously. One thing I always worked on was remembering first names and something of importance to the person. The next time we met I would greet them personally by name and ask them something about them. I have always been conscious of greeting everyone with a smile and positive attitude, even if something wasn't going right, which was important to me.

Owning my own business and having the freedom of time, I was still searching for the freedom of income, so I started to look for something with a residual income. In 2008 I was introduced to Organo Gold, a healthier coffee company. I did not drink coffee at the time, but I did have my business hat on and knew that the masses did drink coffee multiple times a day. If I only had to introduce them to a healthier brand, that to me was genius, so I decided within the hour that I would start a part-time venture. Who would have imagined the lessons I have learned along the way from building teams and the lives that have been impacted around the world. It is rewarding to know that each person is working towards his or her dreams and in order to achieve mine, it is imperative that I help others.

In 2009 I was reintroduced to the book Think and Grow Rich. The Napoleon Hill Foundation and Organo Gold formed a formal, exclusive, lifetime partnership. Both organizations have missions to make the world a better place, which makes it such a powerful and profitable partnership.

In 2011 my husband and I chose to move to an area where I was raised to raise our children. It was a dream of mine to move closer to family and enjoy a lifestyle of mountains, lakes, and warm weather. I was excited because we were changing lifestyles and, at the same time, I was fearful of going out and meeting people again.

With that dream came some adversity and the company that I had operated for over seventeen years ended. My contracts had expired as it was important to my clients to have a local contact. Here I was again starting over in a community where I did not know anyone. It was important that I get out and network in the community groups and meet others but something was holding me back.

I was busy all the time, and had the energy to get things done, move a great distance away, change our home, the kid's schools, friends, and work and then it hits me! Maybe moving wasn't a good choice. Why do I feel the way I feel? I am so tired. I am crying all the time. I can't get out of bed. I just want to sleep. What is happening to me? I had been a night owl and a go getter, and now I was in bed at 8 pm?

I started to feel very tired, and I can remember not wanting to get out of bed. I had a three and six year old and both were busy and around me constantly and yet I just could not move my body. My mind would be telling me to get out of bed, but my body was exhausted. I would sleep a lot. I would get up at 7:00 am, get the kids off to school and preschool and then be back in bed by 8:30 am to sleep until 11:00am. I would get up for a few hours then nap again at 3pm, and then be back in bed at 9:00 pm and do it all again the next day.

This was not me!

I had been to the doctors and had several tests, one of them being a thyroid test, which came back normal. Doctors would said nothing was wrong, so I carried on for another six months. On day, I was at my local dentist and he was doing a check up and felt around my neck and he noticed I was very swollen.

I knew something was not right. I had been training for an obstacle 10 km run and would run four times a week. I was eating healthy, doing strength training and I was still not losing any of the baby weight that I had gained from my pregnancy. My hair was falling out, my eyebrows were thin, my nails were brittle, and my mood swings were frequent. I knew this was not me. I had always been a happy, positive person.

My mind and body knew that something was not right, and I needed to be persistent and find the answers, while at the same time using a positive mental attitude to move forward.

After my dentist said that my neck was quite swollen, I went back to my doctor and she said it was probably just a couple of nodules and sent me for an ultrasound. It turned out that I did have a few nodules in my neck and one of them was quite large in diameter, which concerned the doctors. The next step was to have a biopsy on the large mass. The biopsy came back inconclusive and I asked the doctor what that meant. He said that they were unable to determine whether the mass was cancerous or non cancerous. WHAT??

So what do we do now?

Immediately after the inconclusive results came back I was sent to see a specialist. In that meeting he recommended that we remove my thyroid, or take the nodules out, because if it was cancerous it could continue to grow and I would not be able to see it taking place.

Three weeks later I was in surgery, a day after my son's 8th birthday.

Getting ready for the surgery was one of the hardest parts, and I used pure willpower to create a positive mental attitude. Once you become a mom you not only think about yourself, but you think about your children. I did not know if there would be complications after surgery and so numerous things ran through my mind. I did not know if I would have a voice after surgery, so I sang the kids their bedtime songs into their iPads so they could always hear me sing to them at night. My voice was how I communicated to my team and customers. How would I earn an income if something happened? What kept me going during this process was studying Napoleon Hill's 17 principles of Personal Achievement. I was to be going to Italy for the classroom sessions, even though I was having surgery in August. I determined that, no matter what, I would be travelling to Italy in October to complete my study. I kept a strong positive mental attitude and determined in my mind that everything would go well. I told the doctors that I would be going and the surgery went well. I was able to go to Italy and spend time with the incredible individuals who attend The Napoleon Hill Foundation certification trips. It was an experience I will always cherish. I am grateful for the mentorship of Ms. Judith Williamson. She is inspiring to learn from, and displays her passion for the teaching of the principles every time I see her.

I joined the smiling sisters club! My thyroid was sent off to be examined and I was on my way to recovery, so I thought. About six weeks later, I was called into my doctors' office for the results. I can remember them looking at me and saying...Oh it's all good...Oh wait – I am terribly sorry, they did find a cancerous mass on your thyroid. Wait...did you say the C word? I sat there stunned, looking at him wondering if this was a dream. I am too young to have cancer I thought. I had two young boys, and so much more to do with my life. The doctor told me that I would be referred to an oncologist and they would determine the next step.

In adversity appears the seed of an equivalent benefit in every defeat you experience. You can see it as a loss, or as a chance for gain.

After visiting the oncologists, and hearing what they had to say, I made the choice to live my life with no regrets. I wanted to spend as much time as possible with my boys and family, and not worry about what others had to say. My goal is to teach my boys the 17 principles of personal achievement and to build a business that would be their insurance policy, should anything ever happen to me in the future.

Am I better? Well my thyroid is out, and I am now on medication for the rest of my life. Having a thyroid challenge is a silent disease. Folks around you don't know what you're going through and it's hard to express what you're experiencing.

Our journey to success is usually solitary, yet we are not really alone when we unite with like-minded individuals who have dreams and goals similar to ours. That is how we are able to tap into a higher intelligence for solving problems. The trek toward our goal becomes smoother, takes less time, and feels more peaceful.

I surround myself with like-minded individuals and I am grateful every day for those who have made an impact in my life. A key principle of Napoleon Hill's is the Mastermind Alliance.

Why not make the choice to consider studying the 17 principles of personal achievement through the Napoleon Hill World Learning Centre and join with all the others as they have shared their stories within this book?

I am on the road to recovery, and I used, and still use, an affirmation that continues to help heal my life. A favorite of mine is from Emile Coue, the French psychologist, who gave us a simple but practical formula for building a PMA and maintaining a health consciousness *"Every day, in every way, I'm getting better and better"*.

Ponder this thought for moment - We have two envelopes in front of us. One is filled with positives and one with negatives. You have the choice to choose which envelope you open up daily.

I encourage you to try this little exercise. Fill your envelope with positive sayings and affirmations that you collect from magazines, books, and mentors. At the beginning of the week, pull one of those thoughts or affirmations from the envelope.

Focus on that positive thought for the week and repeat it many times a day until it is picked up by your subconscious and watch the results that take place.

I am stronger because I have made the choice to study Napoleon Hill's 17 principles of personal achievement. I am a stronger woman, mother, daughter, friend and most of all I am a stronger ME.

Having a positive mental attitude helped me through my obstacles and adversity in 2013, and I continue to ensure I maintain a PMA through my journey.

I am here to inspire and help others to see the best in themselves, and to share with them the gift I received from Ms. Noad of being awarded a scholarship to study and become a Napoleon Hill Foundation Certified Instructor.

I have been able to put the teachings to use with my work as a Happiness Coach and I look forward to the future of helping others work towards *"Living Life with an A+PMA"*.

Live, Love, Laugh- I am going to grab a cup of my healthy coffee. Maybe one day we can have one together! Remember that a Positive Mental Attitude attracts success!

Bio

Shannon McVagh-Janz – married and a mother of 2 boys living with an entrepreneur's heart and always creating new ideas. Starting out in the Tourism industry as a certified Resort and Hotel Management graduate and moving into a passion as a certified Event Planner has kept me busy over the last 2 decades.

Now in a position to help others to learn, grow and see the best in themselves!

Learning from those who have gone before us and who have dealt with challenges of a work and home life balance is all part of the journey to be the woman I choose to be!

facebook.com/shannonmcvaghjanz

When The Student Is Ready...
The Teacher Will Appear

By Alexander Alfaro

It was 1999; I was 23 years old and had graduated from college with a Bachelor degree in International Business. It was in that very year that I was first introduced to *"Think and Grow Rich"* by Napoleon Hill, given to me by Robby Thone, one of two owners and Vice President of Diversified Transportation Services. DTS is a logistics brokerage out of Torrance, California and provided my first job opportunity out of college. Roland Sunga, a very good friend of mine, had been working in sales for them and was doing very well. I saw what he had and how he was living, and looked up to him. Naturally, I jumped on the opportunity when he opened the door for me at DTS. Looking back, he was always my *pacemaker.*

Roland and I had originally met in 1993 at Maritz Marketing Research, my first job out of high school. We did phone surveys. You know those people who call you at 6 p.m. after a long day at work just as you are sitting down to eat dinner with the family? That was me. Talk about *learning from adversity and defeat.* Try working eight hours in an attempt to get people to do 30-minute surveys with you, especially when it's about the types of grass they like best on golf courses. We got accustomed to the sound of the phone click followed by a dial tone.

By keeping a *positive mental attitude* I made the best of the job and it actually became fun, learning some valuable communication skills and toughening the skin along the way. Roland and I became very good friends; he had always looked out for me like an older brother. Every time Roland moved up at Maritz, he made sure I was promoted as well. At the time he left the company he was a shift supervisor and on his last day, he made them promote me to take his place. I remained in that position through college, continuing until the week after I graduated and that's when he looked out for me once again, bringing me over to work with him at DTS.

The job was inside sales and I was only given a salary for three months. After that it would be commission only. While going to college I never thought I would eventually be in sales, but little did I know that I was in training during all those years doing phone surveys. Within the first three months I broke all company records and was ready to go on full commission. The day it became official and I became an independent contractor, Robby Thone handed me a copy of *"Think and Grow Rich"*. I read it once and set it down; I wasn't ready and it didn't resonate. I was young, making money, and thought I knew it all.

I was immediately clearing $5,000 to $7,000 per month on full commission and soon forgot what it took to get there. I began to only work four-hour days, spending the rest of the time either at the gym or out partying and having fun with my friends. There was no *budgeting of time and money* so even though I was making a good wage, I still found a way to get myself into a boatload of debt. In 2004, at the height of the real estate market, I decided to jump in. I had met a handful of agents who were all making a lot of money, and since I had the extra time I figured why not. I maintained my customers in logistics and had monthly residual checks coming in, so I decided to go full force into real estate.

It was a hot market. I succeeded immediately; it seemed like everyone did. I doubled my income but didn't realize that the debt was doubling as well. It was 2008 and I was on fire, making $15,000 to $20,000 per month. I owned my home and a three-unit rental property in California, and had two single-family rental homes in Texas. I would attend motivational and real estate seminars and read a few self-help books from time to time but just like before, in one ear and out the other. I was doing well. Who needed all the rah-rah material anyway? Obviously still believing I knew it all, my *"Think and Grow Rich"* book remained on the shelf with the rest of the self-help stuff I had been sold on and had accumulated throughout the years.

The crash at the end of 2008 hit me like a Mike Tyson right cross, knocking me out cold. The income disappeared almost immediately, all of the houses foreclosed and the excessive spending and lavish lifestyle ended. Everything was lost in what seemed like a few short months. My debt was now over $100,000 and there was no way to pay it back. I did what I could in real estate in 2009 and made enough to simply survive. My wife, son and I had to move in with my brother-in-law, sharing a bedroom in a two-bedroom, 900-square-foot house. Struggling to make ends meet while having an enormous amount of debt and nothing promising in sight became my rock bottom.

In the beginning of 2010 I reached out to an old friend, Ryan Renee, whom I had met at Diversified Transportation. He had started his own company, which had recently been bought out by what is now one of the largest brokerages in the U.S., Echo Global Logistics. With my tail between my legs, I asked Ryan to bring me on in inside sales with a draw of $2,500 per month. Basically it was an advance on any commission I would earn. Funny thing is, although Ryan knew I had been making a killing in real estate, he always told me to make sure to not let logistics go. I never listened and had lost every client I had. Listening to wise sage council was never my strong point.

When I started at Echo, one of the agreements we made required me to go into the office and work eight-hour days, something I had not done for a very long time. This was the first time I had worked under someone and had to be somewhere by a certain time every morning since my first job out of high school. It was an hour-and-a-half drive each way in bumper-to-bumper traffic. If you have ever driven in Los Angeles, you know exactly what I am talking about. I hated it; it contributed to the negative mental attitude that I had acquired during the downward spiral to the bottom. On a positive note, it was steady income, helping to pay the bills and put food on the table.

Then one day out of the blue, my miracle happened. No, I didn't win the lottery and become an instant millionaire. It was even better. I simply woke up and decided to change my mental outlook and attitude. I knew I had to do the drive regardless, so I figured I might as well be productive with that time. I grabbed the box of self-help audio books I had accumulated over the years and began listening on my daily commute. It became my routine; half the time I listened and half the time I daydreamed about all the things I wanted and knew I could have. It was always on and I was constantly listening to positive words on my daily drive. I listened to everything I could get my hands on, my confidence grew and I developed a *positive mental attitude.* I avoided the negative news, and TV altogether, and started to filter out negative people and their negative energy. I started to get back into shape. I felt healthy and strong, and that feeling of faith in what I could do started to return. Many hours of audios later, there was one thing that stood out to me the most. Everyone seemed to be regurgitating the same material and simply packaging it in their own way to make it seem unique. I realized I had heard it all before, and it was material I had read over 10 years ago.

In mid-2012 I picked up *Think and Grow Rich* once again, and began to read. Twelve years after receiving the copy for the first time, I learned that when the student is ready, the teacher will appear. This time the words sent chills up and down my spine along with a feeling of unworldly peace in my heart and understanding ... ***thoughts*** *are things ... you get what you* ***think*** *about most ... whatever the* ***mind*** *of man can conceive and believe, it can achieve.* It was all hitting home ... with every adversity, every failure and every heartache comes the seed of an equivalent or a greater benefit. The one thing that stood out the most and hit home the hardest was a discovery that Mr. Hill had made when he did an analysis of over 25,000 successful people. He said that men who succeed in an outstanding way seldom do before the age of 40 and more often, they do not find their real place until well over 50. I immediately went from feeling as if I was running out of time or that my time had already passed, to realizing I was just getting started!

I was 37 years young. This shift in mindset altered everything about my thinking process. I read the book over and over, and listened to the audio book over and over. I had developed an unbeatable positive mental attitude and I had faith that something good was on its way. A few short months after the shift in mindset, I received a phone call from the regional director at a Seattle-based logistics company. He wanted to sit down with me to discuss an opportunity to help open an office in Los Angeles. I had been referred to him by one of the fathers on my travel baseball team. The entire time I was struggling financially I was managing my son's travel baseball team. It was a second job without pay, but my love for the kids and the game was the only reward I needed. Little did I know the *law of increasing returns* was in effect and my involvement with the team would pay me back tenfold. I thought... wow, this stuff really works. You get what you think about, and out of nowhere I had an offered salary of $10,000 per month, which I obviously took.

My failures with money made me a lot smarter in managing it. I created a plan to pay off all of my debt. I no longer craved any of the material things. The newfound money was great but I still felt I was missing something. I still had someone to answer to, a boss, and I was missing that freedom I once enjoyed that truly made what I did a *labor of love*. After six months I was able to put away a little seed money and in December of 2012, I decided to move on and start my own company.

SCL Group started in January of 2013, the very month I came across the Napoleon Hill Foundation website. This is where I discovered his book, *The Laws of Success*, and learned of the 17 principles for the very first time. I truly believe there is an energy flow associated with the book, *Think and Grow Rich*, and I carry it with me everywhere I go, but the best decision I ever made was to engage and study the 17 Principles. In December of 2013, I ordered the *Your Right to be Rich* course and started on the material immediately, forming a small mastermind group that would meet weekly and discuss the material. I made a decision that I wanted to go through the entire journey, not so that I could teach the material but to simply learn it. I paid for the online course and had a minor purpose to attend the next leader certification in which I would be eligible in French Lick, Indiana.

Less than two months after I made that decision and set my goal to finish the journey, I landed two very large accounts that altered my financial picture in a major way. I don't believe in luck; we create our own luck but there is truly *infinite intelligence* there to back us up if we have the right mental attitude. Napoleon Hill stated, *"When riches begin to come they come so quickly, in such great abundance, that one wonders where they have been hiding during all those lean years"*. The minor purpose I had set to engage and learn the principles, and the positive mental attitude I worked hard daily to maintain, opened up the doors and allowed for infinite intelligence to do its job. This happened within two months of setting that minor purpose! Since then I have paid off all of my debt and I do not owe a cent to anyone. It's an amazing feeling. I now have five sales reps working for me, all required to read *Think and Grow Rich* and all must learn the 17 *Laws of Success*.

My chief aim is to create SCL Youth Mastermind, which will be designed to teach the principles of success and the self-discipline needed to master the body and the mind. The goal is to have a step-by-step plan for obtaining Napoleon Hill's 12 Riches of Life. When you think of riches, the first thing that comes to people's minds is money, but that's actually the last thing on Mr. Hill's list and the least important. We live in a society enamored by money and the meaningless material things it can buy. There's a country song by Kristian Bush called Trailer Hitch that sums it up perfectly. "You can't take it with you when you go; I've never seen a hearse with a trailer hitch." If it's not money, what is it? It's something that for me took all the struggles, the defeats and the adversity to achieve. A positive mental attitude is the first and most important aspect of the 12 Riches of Life. We are surrounded by continuous waves of negativity and if we allow ourselves, we can be swallowed up and dragged into the sea to drift aimlessly without purpose. The earlier youth can get their hands on this material and learn how to maintain *PMA (Positive Mental Attitude)*, the better.

Now I am not delusional and think that I can get through to everyone at an early age. It simply doesn't work that way. I know that when the student is ready, the teacher will appear. They will go through the ups and downs of life, as we all do, but at least we can plant that seed of the importance of a positive mental attitude and give them a basic understanding of the laws of success. We can teach them to always look for the seed of an equivalent or greater benefit every time they stumble, and most importantly let them know they are just getting started, just as I am.

Bio

Alexander Alfaro is the CEO and founder of SCL Group. A Supply Chain and Logistics Consulting Firm. He is the Chief Logistics Consultant for SCL Group, Personal Fitness Trainer through The National Academy of Sports Medicine, and soon to be Napoleon Hill Certified Instructor and Leader. Throughout his study of Napoleon Hill's Success Philosophy he was able to turn adversity and failure into success and SCL Group is now a multi-million dollar revenue firm. Inspired by Napoleon Hill's *"Think and Grow Rich"*, *"The Law of Success"*, and Hill's 12 Riches of life he formed SCL Mastermind Group. SCL Mastermind focuses on PMA (Positive Mental Attitude), #1 on Hill's 12 Riches of Life list. SCLM preaches doing the right things on a daily basis to keep the mind positive and away from the negative energy that surrounds and can consume us daily. Inspiring daily growth by reading positive books and listening to positive audios, setting goals, eating healthy, getting/keeping fit, but most importantly...knowing what you want, walking with expectancy, living in the moment, and feeling good NOW.

You Matter: Mine Your Mind

By Brenda Dear

THE YEAR I turned fifty I caved to the lie that since I had not become a published author it was too late. Then I came across Brendan Gill's book Late Bloomers in which he looks at 75 remarkable men and women whose greatest achievements occurred, or were recognized, in the second half of their lives. Gill pays tribute to one of my most inspirational muses; the late Karen Blixen, who died in 1962 the year after I was born. I was first introduced to Karen Blixen when I stumbled across one of her most famous quotes:

> *"Difficult times have helped me to understand better than before how infinitely rich and beautiful life is in every way and that so many things that one goes around worrying about are of no importance whatsoever."*

1965 – A FOUR YEAR OLD'S ACCOUNT OF HURRICANE BETSY

Born January 1, 1961, the youngest of seven children, I have vivid memories from the 1965 devastation of Hurricane Betsy. Hurricane Betsy is infamously known as "Billion Dollar Betsy" because it was the first storm to cause damage in excess of one billion dollars. When Betsy was done with the Louisiana coast, more than seventy-six people were dead and thousands homeless. As a four year old, I remember National Guard tanks with bullhorns warning citizens of the mandatory evacuation ordered by local and national officials. We were a family of nine living in public housing and my dad, a Navy veteran, removed the bedroom doors from their hinges. We managed to use the doors to float to higher ground in order to evacuate and escape death by drowning. As we were floating on the old wooden doors, my tender eardrums heard a piercing scream. The New Orleans landscape is filled with manhole covers used to access sewer pipes for inspection and maintenance, and because of Hurricane Betsy's storm surge, many lids were blown off. As I braced my tiny body to peer over my makeshift floating device I soon learned that one of the manhole covers had blown and my mom was being sucked into the vortex of swirling flood waters. The chaos of grabbing mom out of the swirling flood waters was over as quickly as it had occurred, and the shock left me more numb than afraid.

1969 – AN EIGHT YEAR OLD'S ACCOUNT OF HURRICANE CAMILLE

We barely rebounded from Hurricane Betsy in 1965 when Hurricane Camille came calling in 1969. I was so devastated by the repeat trauma of flood waters I became bitterly resentful of my flood prone city. I loathed the bowl-shaped city of New Orleans during hurricane season, which is typically June-November, but found it fascinating during the rest of the year. Blistering hot summers were the worst for me. Summer after summer the neighborhood kids would turn on the fire hydrants to play and cool off in the raging waters. As a result, I spent a lot of hot summers in the hot house. In my own mind, I was a young survivor of the devastating horrors of Hurricanes Betsy and Camille whose fears were being marginalized. Because I stayed indoors so much, I heard way more grown up conversations about our financial struggles than any kid should ever have to hear. I grew up with insecurities that no one took seriously so I began to internalize my emotions.

1978 – GOODBYE HIGH SCHOOL – HELLO UNIVERSITY

I graduated from high school early and was the first to complete university, although a few of my siblings started but didn't complete the endeavor. I qualified for the maximum Pell Grant for college, and worked part-time at Dixie Brewery, which was leveled after Hurricane Katrina, and was able to buy myself a used car. My oldest sister, Coritha, had become my closest role model and confidant and gave me hope for a brighter future. Coritha was affectionately known as Rita and she taught self-sufficiency, the importance of getting a good education and having a stable career. Rita finished Dental Hygiene School and later tried her hand at cosmetology, eventually managing a Floral Shop. She had a great artistic eye and I remember spending summer nights in her beautifully decorated home. Rita had a wonderful husband, two beautiful children and a huge mocha caramel colored Irish setter named Rocky.

December 1983 I graduated from, and accepted a full-time job at, Xavier University of Louisiana. In May 1984 I married my childhood sweetheart. I wore Rita's wedding dress and her fireplace was the backdrop for my cherished wedding photos. Her wonderful husband Irvin walked me down the aisle. Rita had been battling cancer but showing signs of a great recovery and possible remission. Although she wasn't completely well, her courage and strength was iron clad; indicative of the women in my bloodline. A small reception followed my short wedding and it was catered by the famous Leah Chase at Dooky Chase Restaurant.

In May 1985 I gave birth to my first son. I learned patience and courage from Rita and was devastated when six months after the birth of my son she lost her battle with cancer. Rita was the one person who seemed to understand my insecurities, and genuinely cared about my lofty dreams of a better life. My anguish, fear, and resentment, took me back to my younger reclusive days. I can remember accompanying my niece Florence to the funeral home to get her mom's body ready for burial. It took all the strength inside of me to pretend I was as strong and confident as my teenage niece. I was boiling mad with bitter, selfish, anger because I was still a scared little girl who desperately needed her big sister Rita.

In February 1993 salt was added to my wounds. I was still suffering when my dad disappeared and was found dead. I who urged my brothers, who had been searching for days for him, to go to the morgue. Mom sued the city because we later learned that Dad had fallen while exiting the city bus and the city failed to report the accident. Apparently, someone called the ambulance and dad somehow arrived at the hospital without his wallet. Dad always kept money in his wallet so my guess was someone helped themselves to the money and tossed the wallet. Although a veteran, dad never wore a dog tag, so determining his identity and next of kin never happened. After claiming dad's body, we decided to have him cremated. My brother Robert was the only African American riverboat Captain at the time and his boss allowed him to spread dad's ashes at sea. We had a somber ceremony and I could tell my brothers were devastated. For weeks they hardly spoke of the horror of finding dad among the John Doe's waiting to be claimed in the city morgue.

2005 – FORTY YEARS AFTER HURRICANE BETSY

August 28, 2005 is a date etched into the psyche of tens of thousands of people in and outside of Louisiana. The trauma of Hurricanes Betsy and Camille were memories long suppressed until Hurricane Katrina came creeping like a spider and left whirling like a school of great white sharks. Ironically, the devastation of Hurricane Betsy led to the creation of the US Army Corps of Engineers' Hurricane Protection Program, which provided for New Orleans protection levees that unfortunately failed 40 years later during Hurricane Katrina. New Orleans natives had survived so many hurricanes but this time their complacency and refusal to employ accurate thinking proved fatal to many. Fortunately, families that could evacuate did so and safely made it to my home in North Carolina.

My own family had already survived major flooding from Hurricane Juan in 1997, the year before relocating to North Carolina. My mother was both widowed and experiencing declining health. She had survived losing her husband and first born daughter to a long battle with cancer. For years I questioned my decision to relocate, especially as my mother's health declined.

Sadly, Hurricane Katrina brought more devastation to my frail aging mother. Mom was 75 years old and, days after Hurricane Katrina, she suffered a mild stroke. Contributing factors were not just the loss of material possessions, she also had two sons missing for several days after Hurricane Katrina. One son was a riverboat captain whose job required him to pilot a riverboat out of the city of New Orleans to a dry dock. The other son was a foreman for the local water municipality and stayed in New Orleans to supervise the sandbagging efforts. The worry took a toll on mom's health and, as the news of long-term devastation to the city of New Orleans mounted, mom became more and more withdrawn. A local doctor-treating mom feared that medication would only mask her symptoms and felt being in North Carolina rather than in New Orleans was the real root of her declining health. In the end, after settling back home, mom learned she had breast cancer, underwent a mastectomy and, as of this writing in 2015, remains cancer-free.

2007 – SADNESS AFTER THE MOVIE

Mom though unable to return to her home in New Orleans insisted on moving back with my second eldest sister Marie whose home just outside of the city of New Orleans had been repaired. Marie was affectionately known to many as Tiny because she had the tiniest legs. She was both blessed and cursed to have worked her Old Navy job while temporarily living with me in North Carolina. Blessed to have employment when so many others didn't but cursed because Tiny was in no emotional and physical state to work her 8-10 hour a day retail management job. She hardly had time to process her loss or even deal with the insurance companies and other affairs of rebuilding her life. On one occasion Tiny nearly collapsed on the job requiring the ambulance to be called.

Fortunately paramedics were able to attend to her and she heeded their suggestion and took a few days off to rest. We later learned that Tiny had been previously diagnosed and prescribed medication for hypertension, which was exacerbated by stress. Because Tiny didn't like the side effects from the medicine she failed to take it as prescribed for the early warning signs. When she return to her home right outside of New Orleans she quickly settled back into her job at Old Navy while overseeing a few minor home repairs. One added responsibility however was the care of Mother, which was quite frankly another full-time job.

Just shy of six months later Deen, who had been Mom's primary caregiver returned to her home in New Orleans, and out of necessity resided in a trailer on the property to better oversee reconstruction. Mid-2007 the home was repaired and Mom moves back into my sister Deen's home. A few months later I returned home for a visit to celebrate Deen's 1st Thanksgiving back in her home since the devastation of Hurricane Katrina. On the evening of Thanksgiving us girls (mom, Tiny, Deen and me) decided to see the movie Last Holiday which proved to be an hour filled with laughter and silliness. We sat as closest to the big screen as I had ever done and we laughed until tears ran down our face. Sadly, that same evening about 4 hours later we received a call that Tiny was dead. When we arrived at Tiny's home she was still dressed in her movie attire with one stalk difference; Tiny was lying motionless in the doorway of her bedroom as though asleep.

HUMANITY'S MOST BENEFICIAL POWER: ACCURATE THINKING

As I reflect on surviving Hurricanes Betsy & Camille first-hand at age 4 and 8 respectively, and surviving Hurricane Katrina second-hand at age 44, I am grateful for the knowledge and application of Dr. Napoleon Hill's principle of *Accurate Thinking* to aid me on my journey back to spiritual and emotional stability. Accurate thinking is critical as we focus on why we exist, and how our human existence fits into the grand scheme of humanity. It begs the question – "What should I do in this life so that my living is not in vain. The only way to answer such a tough question, in my opinion, is to study, embrace and apply of Dr. Napoleon Hill's 17 Principles of Success. I did not mind sacrificing and enduring hardship, but I allowed my willingness to serve others distract me from my ultimate reason for service, which is Jesus himself. I neglected genuine quiet time with my Creator, and reading of His word.

Dr. Napoleon Hill's 17 Principles of Success has inspired me to dig deep down and decades back into a tempestuous childhood filled with fear, insecurities, poverty and the trauma of having survived multiple life altering New Orleans Hurricanes. Dr. Napoleon Hill says, "the mind is the greatest of all man's assets, yet it is often the least used and the most abused". He concludes that, "because all ideas are conceived through thought, *accurate thinking* is the most beneficial power available to man". My life is a living testimony to Hill's assessment that thought-habits come from either one of two sources: physical heredity and social heredity. Hill's definition of *Physical heredity—one inherits from this source something of the nature and character of all the generations of the human race, which have preceded him. Accurate thinking, however, can modify a great deal of it.* Hill's definition of *Social heredity--consists of all environmental influences, education, experience and impulses of thought produced by external stimuli. The greater portion of all thinking is inspired by the influence of social heredity.*

My physical and social heredity served as limitless demons for years as they deprived me of the ability to think accurately. Where I should have drawn strength from my heredity, I drew discontentment. Instead of pride and gratitude, I drew sadness and bitterness. Through Hill's teachings, I learned that the most commonly expressed negative emotions, and the more dangerous, are: fear, hate, anger, jealousy, revenge, vanity and greed. These negative emotions he said were the seven robber barons which often deprive men of their opportunity of achievement because they make *accurate thinking* impossible.

In the depth of my depression it was hard for me to pray but, in allowing myself to just cry out in anguish, my tears and supplications became my prayer. I had to learn to be intentional about being a victor and living a life of purpose. I have had this story in my heart and soul for decades but never the boldness and faith to trample fear and pride to expose my frailties. I pray my story inspires you and brings solace on your journey to control your thoughts, emotions and, ultimately, your actions toward a *life that matters.*

Bio

BRENDA M. DEAR, MSOD, SHRM-CP
Founder and CEO of DEAR HR Consulting and Coaching, LLC; focusing on 21st century HR best practices, coaching for continuous improvement and pipeline creation of next organizational servant leaders. Community advocate for young people aging out of foster care or juvenile justice systems. Certified HR professional and recent IBM Corporation retiree. Prior to retirement served as Global Diversity Workforce Partner where she consulted with Senior Executives, Recruiters, and extended HR teams providing *workforce strategies and project management.*

Currently an International Exchange Coordinator with EF High School Exchange Year (EF). Certified by EF and the US Department of State Brenda is responsible for placing exchange students in American homes and schools and monitoring the student's safety and progress during their stay.

Currently a Napoleon Hill Certified Instructor candidate. Brenda holds an EO Compliance Certification, BA in Political Science, and an MS in Organizational Change and Leadership. She also serves on several educational and nonprofit boards in her local community. *She can be reached on LinkedIn, Twitter: IAMBRENDADEAR, Facebook: Brenda Mitchell-Dear*

Eradicating Poverty in Nigeria via the Propagation and Adoption of Napoleon Hill's Success Principles

By Ore Ohimor

Nigeria and the Paradox of Poverty

Nigeria, a former British Colony, became an independent nation in 1960. Its population is estimated to be about 170 million. This makes it the most-populous black nation in the world. It is home to over 250 ethnic nationalities who are mainly Christians, Muslims, and adherents of African Traditional Religion. Nigeria has emerged as Africa's largest economy, with 2013 GDP estimated at US$ 502 billion.

Nigeria is a major producer and exporter of Oil and Gas, with daily oil production of about 2.3 million barrels daily. However, sadly, it suffers from a shortage of refined oil products such as petrol, and diesel, as well as massive power outages. It is characterized by weak institutions, especially public institutions, which are wracked by endemic corruption resulting in very poor service delivery to its citizens. This is evidenced in the fairly dismal statistics relating to key social and economic indicators such as poverty and unemployment, insecurity, a life expectancy of 52 years, and high maternal and infant mortality.

What is Poverty?

"Fundamentally, poverty is a denial of choices and opportunities, a violation of human dignity. It means a lack of basic capacity to participate effectively in society. It means not having enough to feed and clothe a family, not having a school or clinic to go to, not having the land on which to grow one's food, or a job to earn one's living, and not having

186

access to credit. It means insecurity, powerlessness, and exclusion of in-dividuals, households and communities. It means susceptibility to vio-lence, and it often implies living in marginal or fragile environments, without access to clean water or sanitation" (UN Statement, June 1998 – Signed by the Heads of all UN agencies)

This is why it is especially worrisome that over 62% of Nigeria's 170 million people live in extreme poverty.

The Paradox

This dismal situation is however countered by the following ironic facts - Nigerians are some of the most highly educated people in the world, with several PhDs and scholars in various disciplines including Sciences, Technology, Engineering and Mathematics (STEM), Law, and Arts.

For example, In 2013, though making up less than 1 percent of America's black population, Nigerian Americans—many from modest backgrounds—made up 20 to 25 percent of the black students at Harvard Business School and are starkly overrepresented in America's top invest-ment banks and law firms. (Source: Amy Chua and Jed Rubenfield The Triple Package)

Napoleon Hill Success Philosophy to the Rescue

Napoleon Hill's Success Philosophy is captured in his 17 Success Principles, which include the following:

1. Develop Definiteness of Purpose: The adoption of a Definite Major Purpose and a specific plan for its achievement is the starting point of individual achievement

2. Establish a Mastermind Alliance: An alliance of two or more minds working in perfect harmony to attain a common definite object. Napoleon Hill said "No man can be a permanent success without taking others along with him.

3. Assemble an Attractive Personality: This is a personality dominat-ed by a Positive Mental Attitude (PMA), great Communication

Skills, Sincerity of Purpose, Humility, Promptness of Decision, and Tolerance.

4. Applied Faith: faith is your awareness of, belief in, and harmonizing with the universal powers. Faith is an active state of mind in which there is a relating of the mind to the vital forces of the world or Infinite Intelligence.

5. Going The Extra Mile: The habit of rendering more and better service than you are immediately compensated for.

6. Create Personal Initiative: be a person that is self-directed, i.e. a person who does things that should be done without being told and one who goes the extra mile.

7. Build a Positive Mental Attitude (PMA): A PMA is the single most important principle of the science of success. You must employ it in order to get the maximum benefit out of the other 16 principles.

8. Control Your Enthusiasm: This helps you to change even your negative expressions and experiences into positive ones.

9. Enforce Self-Discipline: This is necessary for controlling your emotions and managing your willpower.

10. Think Accurately: be conscious of the two big mistakes of either believing on the basis of little or no evidence, or the tendency to disbelieve anything you do not understand.

11. Control Your Attention: this is the act of coordinating all the faculties of the mind and directing their combined power to a given end.

12. Inspire Teamwork: Great success requires teamwork, i.e. working with a large group of people in harmony towards a common purpose.

13. Learn from Adversity and Defeat: Remember that you need not accept defeat as failure but only as a temporary event which may prove to be a blessing in disguise.

14. Cultivate Creative Vision: Make a Commitment to create a better future.

15. Maintain Sound Health: Be sound both in Body and Mind.

16. Budget Your Time and Money: Time and Money are scarce resources which require careful management if you are to be successful

17. Use Cosmic Habitforce: In other words, work with the laws of nature to guide you to your success destination

WHY NAPOLEON HILL'S SUCCESS PHILOSOPHY?

The soundness of the research methodology, the veracity of its findings over time and its widespread acceptance, especially as evidenced by the over 60 million books sold, as well as the large number of motivational writers and speakers who have ridden on the back of these teachings to launch their careers over the years. My personal experience with these teachings

As much as I can recall, my first exposure to these teachings was about 1994. This was a challenging time for my country and myself. Nigeria had gone through national elections in 1993 which was throwing up a winner until the results were abruptly annulled by the Military. This led to widespread unrest with debilitating effect on the economy. I was caught up in this situation and ended up losing my business and being bankrupt.

This was a most challenging time in my life. This was especially so since most of my earlier life had been relatively smooth. I had started school at about age 5 which was early but made possible by the fact that my mum was a school teacher, then proceeded smoothly through secondary school and on to the university where I earned a Bachelors and Masters Degrees in Business Administration. I then got my first job working as a Sales Agent, then Sales Executive, and later Marketing Support Manager to Rank Xerox Nigeria (the local subsidiary of the Xerox Corporation) in 1989. I resigned in 1991 to start my own business as a Distributor to Rank Xerox Nigeria. Barely 3 years later, I was broke and searching for answers.

Indeed, as espoused by Napoleon Hill, every adversity carries within it the seed of an equivalent or greater benefit, since during this period, especially with nowhere to go, I got buried in motivational books especially The Bible, Tough Times Never Last, But Tough people Do by Rev Schuller, and Napoleon Hill writings such as Think and Grow Rich, The Master Key to Riches, and Grow Rich with Peace of Mind. I read these books for an average of 8 or more hours daily, usually going out to take walks to exercise and relax my mind only. The beauty of this exercise was the acquisition of a success consciousness which replaced my experience of failure and gave me the courage to make a major career change.

I recall the urgings from the books to search inside of me for my gifts and to dare to start again in a new direction. I decided that I was going to be a Trainer/Consultant. I came to this decision after a careful review of my experience as a Distributor and the fact that I really did not have any competitive edge in light of competing products and alternative sources for customers to obtain the products I sold. We were then left with slashing prices in order to sell, thus reducing drastically our already thin margins. I decided to go into an area that had some barriers to entry and where I could more easily distinguish my offering.

In my moments of deep reflection, I recalled that years earlier I had served as Lecturer on a course organized by a former Classmate during my MBA and the feedback from the participants was very positive. I then decided to be a Trainer/ Consultant for the biggest company in Nigeria - Shell Nigeria, which incidentally operated one of their offices from the town in which I lived. I followed up this decision by initiating contact with some of my contacts in Shell who introduced me to the Officer in charge. I met with the officer who basically revealed that they did lots of their training programs in-house, using internal faculty both in Nigeria and from Shell companies worldwide. Thus there were very limited opportunities for an external trainer especially in the management area.

This was one moment I reached inside and remembered something I had been taught in my MBA class earlier, i.e. every elephant (read as large company) has a weakness, look for its weakness and exploit it. You know most big companies think that they are pretty awesome in their performance. And in fairness to them, they usually are, otherwise they would not have either grown big or remained large.

So I undertook a careful study of this behemoth of a company which, at that time, was producing about 1 million barrels of oil, representing about 40% of Nigeria's total oil production and found an underbelly. Shell was basically a techno-centric company that produced a commodity that buyers were lining up to buy. Its business model was such that its buyers had long-term purchase contracts and these were fulfilled by the loading of Oil Tankers from the Terminals which were remote from the offices. It was basically a seller's market with very minimal human contact with their customers in the traditional sense of the word. So you easily saw that they were not likely to be customer-focused.

This was especially easy for me to see since I had spent all my working and business life previously in Sales and Marketing. I thus proceeded to design and offer them a Customer Service Course which I then christened as Customer Reception Management Course. The name was deliberately chosen because the one area in which Shell dealt with customers was in receiving and handling people (i.e. Contractors, Visitors, and Community Representatives) who came to their offices in course of their business and this became a good place to introduce this new program.

When I tried to sell the idea to the company, the initial answer I got was that they really did not see the need for it since they were not a sales organization in the ordinary sense, and really the challenge was to meet buyer demand and not to recruit new customers. It was then I shared with them a wider definition of the term "Customer" which meant all the people a company has to deal with. Of course such a list included Contractors, Visitors, Community Representatives, and Government Officials. We also knew that the first and last points at which the company dealt with these Customers was at the Gates / Reception Areas of the company. We kept pushing this proposal for another 18 months before we were given an opportunity to test the idea with a first batch of

20 participants. The day we had spent at least 18 months preparing for finally arrived.

It was a 2-day program, which was attended by officials who came to evaluate it. At the end of day one, I was called into the office of the Departmental Manager and informed that they had decided to give me two more sets of participants, making 3 runs of the course. Of course I was ecstatic, since years of preparation had paid off in emotional and financial terms. My faith in my ability to deliver the program, as well as the contribution of our program to the improved performance of our Customer (Shell) had come to pass.

Remember that, in the intervening period I was broke. I was owing rent and could hardly fuel my car. In fact, on the day we started the program, my car broke down and I had to use a taxi to and from the class, however the months of success programming kept me going. My faith in my idea was truly tested, but I believed in it and never wavered. The further icing on the cake was that I was promptly paid by cheque by the end of the second day of training and eventually went on to earn within a week enough money to offset my back rent, fix my car and generally regain control of my financial situation. The benefits of this idea are still unfolding since I have had the opportunity of training over 10,000 staff and over 1000 members of Shell Nigeria host communities in various areas including Customer Service, Personal and Leadership Development, and Conflict Resolution in the nearly 20 years since I ran that first course in November 1995.

Becoming A Lawyer

My next major goal was becoming a lawyer. This decision was influenced by several factors, most of which was my ancestry. My father was a lawyer and from my earliest years people have called me a lawyer, or suggested that I become a lawyer. However, I saw it as people just wanting me to be a clone of my father, and I wanted to be able to chart my own course in life.

In Nigeria it is very common to suggest to kids that they follow their parents' careers, irrespective of whether or not they had the aptitude for it.

My response to these suggestions was to rebel. When it was time to attend the University I decided to study Business Administration and graduated at about 20 years of age. After my compulsory National Youth Service Program, there were discussions about my returning to school to study law, however, my preference was to go on to do a Master of Business Administration (MBA) course. I did that, and completed in 1986 and from there went on to join Rank Xerox Nigeria in January 1987. I then decided to study law by correspondence at the University of London, but there were challenges with foreign exchange money transfers out of Nigeria at the time. At any rate, The Council of Legal Education, which regulates the training of lawyers in Nigeria, decided that law degrees acquired by correspondence courses were ineligible for admission into the legal profession in Nigeria.

This was the situation until I got promoted to Marketing Support Manager of Rank Xerox Nigeria in September 1989 and got really immersed in my job, having been promoted to a job that was 4 steps ahead of my last job level, but a position that was only 3 steps ahead, since there was a rule that you could not be promoted more than 3 job levels at once. So I struggled quite a bit with my new job, which I got into as the youngest person to ever make Manager in Rank Xerox Nigeria at that time. I did however have the support and tutelage of my colleagues, and especially my boss who was the Marketing Manager of the company. My desire to study law had to be put on the backburner since the only way I could become one was to go to school full time. I focused on my job until I resigned to become a Distributor in 1991. Once I started running my business, my focus was to get it up and running and there could not be any thoughts of returning to school.

However, the opening came after my success with the training program for Shell, referred to earlier, and I now decided I could go back to full time school, along with running my business. I thus decided to start law school in 1996, and eventually graduated with a Bachelor of Laws

Degree (LLB) in 2000. I had to attend the Nigerian Law School and got called to the bar (admitted to practice law) in February 2003.

Becoming A Napoleon Hill Certified Leader

As may already be obvious from my story above, I am a lifelong learner who is constantly looking for opportunities to improve myself and also to increase my contribution to my clients and customers. My quest for certification is largely to further my work in the not-for-profit area and to contribute especially to fighting poverty, unemployment, and ignorance in Nigeria.

A large number of Nigerians have wrong ideas about success, and suffer from poverty consciousness and associated negatives, including the 7 basic fears mentioned by Napoleon Hill. These are deep-seated and widely held beliefs that have kept our people down for many years. If we must confront and change them, we must come to such an event with superior alternatives that have been tested and proven. The purveyor of such a message must be grounded and able to withstand the inevitable pushbacks that he will meet.

Since challenging these dominating negative beliefs and enthroning a new set of tested, universally applicable principles would help address the pervasive poverty and negative thinking in the land, and in furtherance of my desire to champion this cause, certification and continuous development in this area is inevitable. In 2012, I became the first Nigerian to become a Napoleon Hill Certified Leader and during my Training Program in Belle Isle, Ireland, I shared my dream to propagate this philosophy in my country.

The Challenge Ahead

How do we organize for the propagation of this philosophy in Nigeria, and demonstrate that it works and has the potential to fundamentally affect our lives as a nation?

REVIEW OF CURRENT REALITY IN NIGERIA

In the absence of any framework for successful living, dominating beliefs about success emphasize the following:

- Close proximity to governmental power and exploiting your position for your pecuniary benefit (corruption and nepotism)
- Belief in rituals and the deployment of magic for acquisition of money
- Membership of cartels, cults and groups of such nature, as a passport to wealth
- It does not matter how you get your money, just get it. Morality is of no importance.
- Most of our people are mired in poverty consciousness and have very limited dreams of subsistence living in a world of so much abundance.

MY INITIAL THOUGHTS IN MEETING THE CHALLENGE

The good news is that, at the time of this writing, we have another certified leader in Nigeria and quite a few others undergoing the training. This will help create partners that I can work with in this effort. For now below are some ideas

- Inculcate training on Napoleon Hill's philosophy in the National Youth Service Scheme (NYSC)
- Partner with Churches and other faith-based Organizations
- Introduce Napoleon Hill's books and materials to prisons, especially as potential tools for reformation and providing direction for prisoners whilst incarcerated and upon release
- Work to include it in the University Curriculum, at least as part of General Studies and/or as an elective course
- Serialization and Commentary in Newspapers

Bio

Ore Ohimor is an Attorney, Arbitrator, Management Consultant and Trainer. He has trained over 12,000 staff of Shell Nigeria and members of Shell Nigeria Host Communities in the last 20 years. He lives in Warri, Nigeria with his wife and three children

WHERE'S THE SEED?

By Tami Jackson

A BURNING, OBSESSIONAL desire will keep you awake at night. As you finally drift off to sleep, it will be the last thing you think about. When you awaken in the morning, it will be the first thought on your mind. As you go about your day, ideas about this obsession constantly come to mind. If your daily activities are not in pursuit of this obsession, it almost becomes a distraction because you can't think of anything else you would rather do than to pursue this obsessional desire!

In 2004 I finally began operating, on a full-time basis, the property management business that took me seven years to establish. Coheia Management Enterprise, LLC operated in the urban community of Trenton, NJ. Along with Coheia Management, I also operated a food distribution and a women's halfway house. Through these endeavors I witnessed first-hand how most people in this community lived a life of struggle, and believed that life dealt them a hand they had to live with. There were many dreams and aspirations, but little-to-no hope for a better future.

After 6 years of operation Coheia Management Enterprise had to be dissolved. The business did not achieve the lasting success that I had hoped for, so I went humbly back to the corporate world. Needless to say, my perception of the corporate work place had dramatically changed. Because I see life through the eyes of an entrepreneur, it is depicted in my conversations with fellow employees. During those casual conversations I made another discovery: The corporate work-place contains quite a few people that have a burning desire for entrepreneurship but have no clue how to make it happen.

At this point in my life, I've witnessed the urban community with dreams and no hope, and the corporate community with aspirations and no guidance. Within my burning desire I feel very strongly that we should always feel **GOoD**, wear our passion, and live our dreams. Because of this belief, along with my discoveries, I adopted a self-imposed title, *"The Entrepreneur Advocate"*.

My Definite Major Purpose, my chief aim in life is: "To establish a business with efficient and effective systems to lead, guide, and instruct working individuals with a burning desire for entrepreneurship to develop a business structure that will allow them to deliver their product or service for profit." Hence, ***Entrepreneur Advocates, LLC.***

Entrepreneur Advocates, LLC is well under way. The Business prospectus is in place, business structure and systems are established, and a few clients are already on the roster. But there is one thing that still needs to be in place... a Mastermind Alliance. After studying Napoleon Hills PMA Science of Success principles, I learned that one of the reasons why my property management business did not succeed was because I did not have a Mastermind Alliance in place.

A Mastermind Alliance is two or more minds working together, in the spirit of perfect harmony, towards the attainment of a specific objective. This is the principle that makes it possible for you to acquire and utilize the knowledge and experience of other people. This is required for the attainment of ANY desired goal in life. It is imperative! Lasting success does not come without a Mastermind Alliance, and I'm going to be sure to establish one for Entrepreneur Advocates.

In November 2014, I entered into a business relationship with a mastermind partner. This is the mastermind alliance for which I had been hoping. For now I'm going to spare most of the details about this partnership but I will say this; we share the same vision, and both have a sufficient amount of knowledge, experience, enthusiasm, and money to contribute to this endeavor. This is a family friend and we are on our way to dramatically changing lives, including our own. Little did I know how much my life would change, and in such a short period of time. Three months into this partnership, and several interactions and transactions later, I realized that I was being scammed. Everything that was shared with me to substantiate this individual and their business, including all documents, were falsified. It was a deliberate act of deception that I failed to recognize until it was too late. The financial cost to me was $75,000. The effect to the rest of my life was nothing other than complete devastation!!!!

Here I am, a single mother of 2 school age boys, the head of my household, the only source of provision, and due to this scam my bank accounts are nearly down to zero! More importantly, my inspiration was down to zero. I was broke and broken! I was scared, nervous, worried, and overwhelmed. I didn't know what to do, and I didn't know where to turn. I was completely empty! I had no direction and no inspiration. It was as if someone had hit SELECT ALL and highlighted all my of dreams, aspirations, desires, passion, goals, knowledge, inspiration and direction, then hit DELETE!!! I didn't think I was capable of being in such a place in my life, but here I was, stripped down to nothing.

Over the course of several days I cried, slept very little, and listened to the voice in my head telling me how bad things were and how much worse they were going to get. This was such an awful space to be in and it was taking its toll on me mentally, emotionally, and physically. I knew the only way for me to move out of that space was for me to move myself, but how? I looked over at my mother's framed picture on the dresser and I immediately thought about meditating. I was so overwhelmed I didn't even think of praying or meditating. Meditation is the place where I meet my Mom, who transitioned several years ago, so looking at her picture reminded me to go to my private spot.

I headed over to my private spot, and as usual I hung a sign on the outside of door that said: "In the **GAP**". The sign let's my family know not to disturb me. This is a place where I go "in between the words" to find silence and partake in **G**od's **A**ppealing **P**resence! I positioned myself to meditate but the voice in my head was still very loud. The mental pictures were replaying the business deal gone wrong, the bank accounts with zero balance, and everything the voice said would go wrong, including the eviction notice that I had just received. Everything around me was trashed and I was really having a hard time going "in between the words" and finding silence. I just fell prostrate and cried out, "Abba, **Where's The Seed?**

Principle 13 – Learning From Adversity and Defeat:
*"Every adversity carries with it the **seed** of an equivalent or greater benefit."* The 13th principle of Napoleon Hill's 17 Principles of Success.

This principle states that every adversity, defeat or disappointment we encounter brings with it a seed or many seeds of goodness, or great opportunities that are equal to or greater than the bad thing that we experienced. However, we must look for, and be able to recognize, the seed(s). Knowing that there is a benefit to our adversity is a great start. Everyone knows that failure and physical pain are parts of nature's common language that she speaks to every living creature[1], and we go through this pain and adversity for a purpose. Every defeat in one manner is made up in another, every suffering is rewarded, every sacrifice is made up, and every debt is paid[2].

Not only must we look for this beneficial seed, but we must also realize that it's a **SEED**. A seed is usually the start of something. Once you recognize the seed you will need to grow it into its full-intended benefit for your life. Look at the late great Nelson Mandela, who was jailed for 27 years for his activism against apartheid in South Africa. During his time in prison Nelson Mandela saw the seed of an equivalent benefit to take control of his own mind and not return racism for racism. It took self-discipline for that seed to flower into his never wavering devotion to democracy, equality, and learning. He later came out of prison to become the first black president of South Africa, making great advances for the country. Nelson Mandela found many seeds of equal or greater benefit in his adversity.

There are 2 main requirements needed to recognize and cultivate the beneficial seed(s) in any adversity: *A Positive Mental Attitude and A Definite Major Purpose in life.*

In order to transmute adversity into success you must have a Positive Mental Attitude (PMA). Your mental attitude will be the key factor that determines the direction your adversity will take you. If your attitude is positive, then you will move along and act with faith, feeling good and believing that things will get better and that your actions will produce your desired results. Faith and a Positive Mental Attitude are twin brothers[1]. And a Definite Major Purpose will assure that you move along and act with definite, clear goals and direction. You will recognize the seed and cultivate it with an expectation.

Back to GAP:

I stayed in the GAP for several hours. It took a while for me to enter into that space of silence that I needed so very badly. I needed to feel happy, peaceful, confident, and guided. I prayed, praised and worshiped; then finally I felt His Presence. After a while I began to hear The Still Small Voice that reminded me of who I am in Him...

"Tami, you are my child and I love you. Before I formed you in the belly I knew you; and before you came out of the womb I sanctified you. *Jeremiah 1:5* I have made you a little lower than the angels, and crowned you with glory and honor. *Psalm8:5* You are complete in Me, and I Am the head of all principalities and power. *Colossians 2:10*

I have given you the power, in the name of my Son, Jesus Christ, to cast down imaginations, and every high thing that exalts itself against the knowledge of Me, and bring into captivity every thought to the obedience of Christ. *2 Corinthians 10:5*

It is very important that you be careful for nothing; but in everything by prayer and supplication and with thanksgiving let your requests be made known unto Me. The peace of God, which passeth all understanding, shall keep your heart and mind through Christ Jesus. *Philippians 4:6-7* So you must forgive and don't worry about anything because vengeance is mine; I will repay, saith the Lord. *Romans 12:19*

Finally Tami, whatsoever things are true, whatsoever things are honest, whatsoever things are just, whatsoever things are pure, whatsoever things are lovely, whatsoever things are of good report; if there be any virtue, and if there be any praise, **think** on these things. *Philippians 4:8* And remember, walk by faith and not by sight. *2 Corinthians 5:7"* Thus Saith The Lord.

Wow! I came out of my private space feeling like I had a burning bush moment! The negative chatter in my head had ceased and I was feeling **GOoD**. I didn't have all of the answers, but I had peace, comfort and a Positive Mental Attitude. When I walked back into my bedroom, I noticed a poster on the wall that listed the 17 principles. I made this poster and put it on my wall several months prior but, on this day, my eyes went straight to it, as if I was seeing it there for the first time. I got closer to read through the list of principles but before I could began reading, these words came into my thoughts: "**Here is your Seed**, the 17 Principles. This is the bridge that will take you from the failure side to the success side of your adversity. This is a seed of opportunity." I was already feeling great, but now I'm really excited. You see, I know I was called to teach Dr. Hill's principles, and there is no more effective way for me to teach these principles then to have applied them in my own life. "Every turning point at which one begins to attain success in the higher brackets of achievement, is usually marked by some form of defeat or failure[1]." Yes, this story is about principle #13, but there is a place for all 17 principles to be applied in an effort to bring me to a place of victory and success.

2 More Seeds:

There are some adversities, defeats and disappointments that bring with it more than one seed of equal or equivalent benefit, and this adversity is definitely one of them. In fact, I think I will be finding seeds from this experience years down the line. But there are 2 additional seeds I'd like to share that I would pay more than $75,000 for. In fact they are priceless.

1) "For we wrestle not against flesh and blood, but against principalities, against powers, against the rulers of the darkness of this world, against spiritual wickedness in high places."

EPHESIANS 6:12

In the beginning I mentioned how there was a voice in my head that constantly told me how bad things were and how much worse they were going the get. Well that voice is one that I am very familiar with and I'm sure you are too. However I can honestly say that I have never experienced the voice in this manner. The voice was very loud, very negative, very persistent and very insistent; so much so that it made me physically sick to my stomach. It put me in mental states that I didn't want to be in, and it tried to get me do things that I did not want to do. Again, familiar, but not to this magnitude. This seed of an equivalent benefit was realizing, **in a big way**, that the battle was in my thoughts. You might say, "duh, Tami!" And I would say, yeah I know, we have this battle everyday. But in a battle of this magnitude, not only did I need to **really know** where the battle was, but I needed to have the proper weapon and understand what it took to win. This was not just any battle, it was a serious outright war! An outright effort to kill, steal and destroy me; and there was nothing subtle about it. It was very blatant and deliberate! I had never experienced this, ever! But once I realized that my struggle was not with the guy who wronged me, the landlord, the bill collectors, or anything I could see or touch, it was the beginning of my victory! And I will say, this was the hardest fight I ever had. But it was also the best lesson and test I've ever had. I may not have aced the test but I damn sure didn't fail! **Strategy:** Always go to the spot within where you feel good. It may be a very, very, very small spot, but you will have one, so go there. Stay there for as long and often as you can and work on expanding that positive space. Have positive thoughts, have a plan, and take positive action.

> "He that dwells in the secret place of the most High
> shall abide under the shadow of the Almighty. I will say
> of the Lord, He is my refuge and my fortress; my God in
> Him will I trust."

PSALM 91:1-2

My relationship with the Lord has always been pretty awesome and I will always look for it to continually evolve. This adversity and the struggle caused me to exercise my faith and experience God in a way that I have never known. What is priceless and cannot be put into words is His vastness and His unconditional love. To feel Him, to know His voice, to watch Him do things on my behalf, and to understand, just a little more, how He sees us! I'm trying to do justice here... There are 26 letters and 5 vowels that make up the entire English language. That just isn't enough to do justice to what I am trying to say. So I'll just say this: The seed to be cultivated here is GRATITUDE!!

THE BLESSINGS:

As the days and months went by, it took a lot of work for me to stay in a positive state. Napoleon Hill once said, "...we have to be <u>forever</u> vigilant of our thoughts for as long as we live". I had to develop strategies, and cognitively implement the 17 principles, particularly principle #7, Positive Mental Attitude. This is part of the journey; seeds are being cultivated, we're walking by faith and not by sight.

While on this journey, God's grace and blessings have helped me stay the course. Five days before I was to go to landlord/tenant court for the eviction, I received a $13,000 check in the mail. I did not have to go to court, and I was able to get caught up on all of my bills. Then within a month following, my accountant informed me that I would be receiving over $23,000 back from my income tax. Shortly after that, I was introduced to, and attended, a much needed business conference, thanks to a dear and longtime friend who financially sponsored me. At that conference I networked with like-minded people and built up my self-confidence to get my business back on track. God is my Conductor and He continues to orchestrate positive movements and people into my life, and my enthusiasm and inspiration has taken new heights.

Because I recognize, embrace and use constructively my blessings, I am better equipped to lead, guide, and instruct working individuals that have a burning desire for entrepreneurship, and help them to develop a business structure that will allow them to deliver their product or service for profit. This is my Definite Major Purpose!

NAPOLEON HILL:

It is the overall plan of the Universe to give man the benefit only of those blessings that he recognizes, embraces and uses constructively[1].

Defeat is never the same as failure unless and until it has been accepted as such[1].

BIO

Tami E. Jackson
Founder and CEO
Entrepreneur Advocates, LLC

Tami Jackson, a professional with over 25 years of business experience in the areas of Information Technology, Project Management, Training, Real Estate Management, Contract and Budget Negotiation, and Business Coaching.

Jackson is a graduate of The College of New Jersey, where she earned a degree in Education. She has a diverse array of skills that has allowed her to gain varied levels of experience in the corporate arena and as an entrepreneur.

In the pharmaceutical industry Jackson worked as an Information Technology and Project Management Professional where she provided training and support to sales forces of over 4000 people. In this same industry she also worked as a Contract Manager, negotiating extensive terms and conditions and multi-million dollar budgets for clinical trials, all while managing staff.

Jackson developed, implemented, and operated a property management company, Coheia Management Enterprise, LLC. Her company managed all aspects of the land-owners property, including leasing, maintenance, and overseeing major renovations. Her skills as a licensed realtor were also used to enhance her business.

Helping individuals reach higher heights is one of Jackson's greatest passions. She is a student and practitioner of Napoleon Hill's Science of Success Philosophy. She is currently the founder and CEO of Entrepreneur Advocates, LLC, a coaching practice where she successfully leads, guides, and instructs working individuals with a burning desire for entrepreneurship to develop their own business structure, allowing them to deliver their product or service for a profit.

To learn more about Tami Jackson and her current endeavors, visit:
www.EntrepreneurAdvocates.com or www.TamiJacksonOnTop.com

If you have a burning desire for a successful business and want to benefit from Tami's growing seeds, send an email to:
office@EntrepreneurAdvocates.com

Meta-Dream brings a new intelligence to change the world

By Takeshi Umemura

I am Japanese living in Tokyo, Japan. Napoleon Hill's philosophy has greatly changed my life. Therefore, I believe his philosophy will continue to improve our future world to come. I remember discovering the book "Think & Grow Rich" when I was 19 years old. At that time, I was suffering from depression because I failed to pass the exam for a university, which I extremely wanted to attend. I decided to study one more year preparing to pass the exam no matter how difficult it would be for me. My heart was burning because passing the exam seemed out of reach for me. I scored an E, which was the lowest rank. I had been getting E scores for the past 3 years in high school.

One day, while walking back home from school, after studying for the exam, I stopped at a local convenience store called Family Mart. As I was shopping I discovered the book "Think & Grow Rich". The book didn't teach me about studying for the exam, but it taught me how to succeed. While reading the book I started following what the book had taught me. I learned the importance of defining my purpose and the importance of helping others.

The greatest know-how that I learned from the book was how to properly use my subconscious mind and the concept of applying the Mastermind principle. It made me discover another power I had never experienced before. On my next exam I raised my score to a C, and then to a B, and finally after many hours and days of studying I raised my score to an A!!! The exam I passed was to enter Tokyo University, which is the most prestigious and difficult university to enter in Japan. This was the start of changing my life for the better by applying Dr. Napoleon Hill's philosophy of success.

At Tokyo University, I wrote a story of drama and dialogue which was expressed by performance of the theater and received champion status among 10 universities for two years. The key to its success was the know-how of applying the Master Mind principle. Growing up I loved doing projects that involved working together with others. Even though we failed some projects, when we succeeded we were very happy to celebrate as a team. I thought this is the happiest feeling to experience and was necessary for me to grow into a leader. I studied science and philosophy at the university. I was selected as the leader of graduates at a graduation ceremony, which was a very exciting achievement for me.

The start of a new career

After graduation, I started a career working with SSI Corporation, which is partnered with The Napoleon Hill Foundation to publicize the philosophy throughout Japan. In time, I became the Instructor for their Science of Success Program. I loved being an Instructor because I could talk deeply with my students. Since childhood, I have enjoyed deep conversations with friends. The world has infinite life experiences all around it. I know I can't experience it all, but I can learn many more while having a deep dialogue together with another person. My ability to work with others and my hard work ethics helped me to become the leader of our sales team. I became #1 salesman of all around Japan for SSI Corporation, and next year, I became manager of the biggest sales team for SSI.

Eventually I was viewed too young to manage elder leaders. I worked very hard during that time as a result it damaged my health. Therefore, I was not able to carry on and I lost my position as manager. Though this was my adversity it came at a good time opening up a way for new things to come. During my life I have experienced some bad injuries and hardships. As a student of Napoleon Hill I was able to overcome them by applying Learning from Adversity and Defeat, Napoleon Hill's 13th Principle of Success.

Same purpose with a new direction

During that time I started my own "Dream Workshop" class with new students. I did this monthly and soon it became popular, gathering more than 50 students for the class. I didn't only have students from Tokyo, but also from other places around Japan. I was happy because I loved to talk deeply with my students and I was able to share my knowledge with others every day.

I quit the SSI Corporation 2009, because I wanted to work on my own purpose and not depending on the company to help me. I wanted to try something new to teach Napoleon Hill principles to more people. What I wanted to do was to teach the principles to the common society more and more and not just with businessmen. I felt Instructors were distanced from their students. I wanted to engage more with people by style of project.

I held workshops and did coaching for individuals and companies at first. I had to work through trial and error. I experienced big failure and separation of partners that I was working with at the time. Even though this happened I wouldn't give up on my purpose because I believed in and applied the success principles in my life. I produced many programs of studying and got #1 sells on the internet at one time. I also did company workshops. Then I created and brought the project of "Orchestra of Education" to a school network company. I was doing many different things during this time in my life.

A miracle event came to me

Then a miraculous event came to me in my life. I discovered a special educational tool named ACHIEVUS in Malaysia. I was traveling with the Napoleon Hill Foundation group for an International Napoleon Hill Convention in 2011. I had come to realize that this game can help others to develop a positive conscious mind and mastermind alliance. It provides an engaging way for people to learn the 17 Principles of Success from children to adults. Achievus was invented by Jeremy Rayzor, which I feel is a real genius. I met him during the morning breakfast at the hotel of Kuala Lumpur, Malaysia. We naturally became good friends quickly.

The year of 2012, I started spreading ACHIEVUS throughout Japan. Many friends helped me to do that delightfully. I thought the spirit of this board game is similar to the Japanese spirit of "Omoiyari" which means being compassionate and considerate of others feelings and needs. This board game helps to inspire people to develop the spirit of teamwork for maintaining a cooperative mind. Achievus is more than playing a fun board game. In actuality it is a cooperative leadership educational tool that provides increased value, the more times it is played. I feel ACHIEVUS is a miracle board game that individuals can experience both as a project and dialogue which I love to experience the most. I believe this is a precious treasure for people to experience and use all around the world.

I founded a company named ACHIEVUS JAPAN, and I developed the group of ACHIEVUS trainers who spread ACHIEVUS and apply the game to their life. I brought Jeremy Rayzor to Japan during 2014. We hosted our first ACHIEVUS convention together with Achievus trainers and guests. It was a delightful experience! Jeremy mentioned during his speech "The mind of ACHIEVUS is America, and the heart of ACHIEVUS is Japan, and the arteries of ACHIEVUS are the ACHIEVUS trainers." Now there are currently 176 ACHIEVUS trainers in Japan. We sometimes hear Win-Win in business is important, not Win-Lose, or Lose-Lose, because Win-Win businesses make both people earn profit. I believe ACHIEVUS is more practical and peaceful, because ACHIEVUS is "Achieve + Us". This concept is not dividing you and I. This doesn't mean a short relationship but means having a deep and long relationship.

Napoleon Hill tells us that the two principles teamwork and the mastermind alliance are different. Teamwork is coordinated with the strength of people working together but a mastermind alliance maintains a state of absolute harmony, which shares a common definite purpose in life among the members. When a mastermind alliance is formed it goes beyond the power of a team from "1+1=2" to an alliance of "1+1+More=5, 6, 7, etc." This concept may be difficult to understand by some people, but we can experience this same state through ACHIEVUS. Playing Achievus is an amazing experience of unity. Almost all games and activities are competitively driven. This competitive drive influences children and most people to feel superior alone when they win over other people. When playing ACHIEVUS we are able to experience a precious feeling of working together to help one another to achieve a common goal. There is even a more added value on top of this, which creates an enormous experience. After playing the game we talk about how we apply Napoleon Hill's 17 Principles of Success in our life. This brings out even more dialogue of new inspiration to come... for us to share!

THE PURPOSE OF META-DREAM

Sharing our inspirations through deep dialogue is called Meta-Dream. I learned about "Meta-Dream" five years ago. Meta-Dream includes many people's dream, but not "Mega-Dream" and not religious. I learned "Dialectics" when I studied philosophy at Tokyo University. Almost all personal opinions have an opposite view, and the situation cannot change at that level. Through deep dialogue, two opposite opinions may be able to blend together as one view. In my experience there are two purposes for dialogue. First, through dialogue we can learn about each other's character. This is very important because people can become angry or sad from misunderstandings. Second, through dialogue, we can think through many aspects. We can discover new ideas together, which can result in many more ideas. I call this idea "Meta-Dream". A Meta-Dream can bring together a new mastermind alliance.

In the world, there are many problems; starvation, economic crisis, war, disparity, a lack of technology, etc. These problems consist of four factors, position, distribution, variation, and application. I think if people all over the world shared deep dialogue and discover Meta-Dream step by step, we can solve these problems and earn an exciting and peaceful world for all. ACHIEVUS is very deep metaphor of this relationship. Who do you think of when you hear the word "US"? Do you think of your friends, family, colleagues, community, your country, or did you think of the people on earth?

If we want to do something valuable to help many people it would be very difficult to do it by yourself. By cooperating with each other, we can do great achievements together. Helping each other beyond our personal power, expanding the circle of "US". Playing Achievus can lead us to our greater-self. Through communication we are able to learn more and more from different perspectives. Actually, ACHIEVUS is a game that we can experience basic adversity through play. The goal of playing ACHIEVUS is not to determine victory or defeat, but the goal is learning to cooperate with each other. Feeling happy together is a special event.

The world is diversified. It requires a higher level of teamwork, which is the "Mastermind" principle. When we play ACHIEVUS, we can learn and discuss together Napoleon Hill's 17 Success Principles to build deep dialogue. The use of such a great tool can gather many people. You can learn about the power of a mastermind by playing ACHIEVUS. I personally will be spreading ACHIEVUS wherever I travel. It is my prayer that the world be filled with more joy and heartfelt smiles. Napoleon Hill's philosophy changed my life and is now improving our future world around "US".

Bio

TAKESHI UMEMURA *is the founder of* *ACHIEVUS JAPAN. He also developed and produced many educational programs, for example, "Math-Mask", "Workshop-Climax", "Four Seasons Sales", "Orchestra in Education", "The method of exciting and success studying". His dream is discovering Meta-Dream involving people all over the world for a happy future.*

Improving the World Through a Positive Example

By Hillary Vargas

"Be the change you wish to see in the world"

- Mahatma Gandhi

Back in 2009 when I graduated from college, I had a vision to change the world through my students and each person I encountered, one at a time. After volunteering with a local organization in Providence, Rhode Island, I realized that my purpose was to work with underprivileged, at-risk youth. Not knowing how, I started on a path of fulfilling my dreams by working at different schools. To my surprise, I discovered a lack of mentoring; no one was showing our youth that there was more to the world outside of their neighborhoods or immediate environment. I then came up with an idea for a lifelong mentorship program to help instill a sense of family that was lacking in many of my mentees' lives.

As I sought ways to launch this project, I came across a book that completely changed my life: Napoleon Hill's *"Think and Grow Rich"*. Reading the 17 principles of success provided a roadmap and foundation that allowed me to pursue my dream. Prior to discovering the book, I thought that the path to success was one that would take me to a high-paying job after college. Thankfully, I eventually came to the conclusion that this was not necessarily the case. I turned down a lucrative job offer after graduation to join Americorps to work in the inner-city schools of Providence for a mere salary of $10,000 a year. While many considered me foolish for doing this, I had discovered that working with underprivileged youth was my passion and my purpose. Success is not always about the amount of income you make, but more often about the difference you make in another person's life.

As I worked to establish the mentoring program with my students, I realized that the very principles that guided me as I pursued my purpose should be passed along to my youth. The fact that Napoleon Hill was a strong advocate for education and believed that the principles he endorsed should be taught in our schools further confirmed this for me. He felt that if "*Think and Grow Rich*" was part of the school curriculum, the majority of students would grow to become successful members of society. Unfortunately, "*Think and Grow Rich*" is not taught in our schools, but I saw the opportunity to pass this incredible knowledge on to my mentees, which I know will make a powerful difference in their lives.

OUR YOUTH IS OUR FUTURE

To this day, I teach and implement the 17 principles in my mentoring program and organization, *Ms. Hillary's Kids*. We are not just any other program; we are a family holding each other accountable. We expect nothing but the best from each other and believe in a commitment to "pass it forward" for generations to come. Our youth is our future. They are our leaders, doctors, politicians, engineers, musicians, entrepreneurs and artists of tomorrow. If we don't believe in them, where will our world be? We must look beyond the exterior and beyond the media and society's portrayal of "urban underprivileged kids".

Having grown up in an urban setting and raised by my single mother who emigrated from Colombia, I used my life experiences to connect with my mentees. I understand firsthand how it feels to always be told what you can't become or achieve versus being encouraged by the message that no dream is too big and the sky's the limit. I believe that with the right mentorship and the right tools, there is nothing that my mentees cannot accomplish.

The mentoring program is designed to help youth establish social, emotional, academic and spiritual balance in their lives. Mentees network with some of the most successful individuals in their respective fields and gain opportunities that enable them to move forward toward fulfilling their dreams. I believe in empowering each of my "kids" to reach for the highest star and in teaching them that they, not their circumstances, determine their futures. In joining Ms. Hillary's Kids, my students are committing not only to themselves, but to their future selves and the effect they will have on the world. They are committing to their peers and to me. They commit to dreaming big, showing up, doing the work and making it happen.

Enjoying the Fruits of Hard Work

Many of my students/mentees are now beginning to see a turnaround in their lives. They're enjoying the fruits of their hard work and the gleaming diamonds of success by applying the many principles taught by Napoleon Hill. One such story is that of Arlene Palma. Prior to joining Ms. Hillary's Kids well over a year ago, Arlene was battling depression and almost succumbed to it. She had forgotten who she was and why she was alive. She actually got to the awful point of standing on the George Washington Bridge with the intention of jumping, BUT God had other plans. Today she uses her story to inspire others. She joined Ms. Hillary's Kids in March 2014 and quickly realized that she had become part of a family that not only saw her true potential but would help her find and follow her true purpose in life. Her dream and purpose is to become a pediatrician who heals children using a more holistic approach. Arlene told me when she becomes a pediatrician she wants her young patients to view her as not only their doctor but also as a mentor. She wants to teach them to slow down and listen to their bodies and use their internal voice to guide their health-care choices.

By following the principles of applying faith, overcoming adversity and defeat, and going the extra mile for others, she has realized her true self. Arlene has changed from someone battling depression into someone who is realizing her purpose and is on the path to achieving her dream. She is now on her way to becoming a medical student. I know she will undoubtedly become that great pediatrician she is meant to be.

FROM SURVIVING TO THRIVING

The next story I'd like to share is that of Hanzel Escorcia. He was born and raised in New Jersey. He grew up with the sense that if he can't feel, he will survive. As a result, his emotions barely existed. With no emotions to remind him that he was human, he slowly entered into depression where all he was surrounded by was emptiness and rage. But he didn't know from where or why. He was 12 when he first realized it would be okay for him to die, he wouldn't care. Days of feeling like that turned to months, then to years. It had been seven years and it seemed to be getting worse. He never thought he would live past 23 years old and decided to live recklessly so he could enjoy the time he had. His brother, who was two years older than him, felt the same way as Hanzel. He struggled as well. But Hanzel felt he was always worse than his brother. And at the end of the day their smiles were fake. Hanzel's plan was he would die at 23, then his brother would last another three years, and then die himself. He believed that was the plan, that is, until November 2015. Hanzel's brother unfortunately committed suicide and Hanzel woke up to everyone just destroyed. But at the same time his brother broke the plan and cut in line in front of him and left. When that happened, Ms. Hillary was there with an open hand and offered Hanzel her mentorship. He is now proud to call himself one of Ms. Hillary's kids. Through the program, he has realized that he has a lot to live for. There are so many goals and dreams that he would like to accomplish.

All his life he had passions that he would have loved to actually explore. However, for most of his upbringing, he always believed that he would never have enough time to experience it all. Now he feels like he has all the time in the world at his fingertips. Hanzel now has plans to go see the world and immerse himself in as many cultures as he can and bring back knowledge of traditions, languages, and most importantly, food. He is currently a college student studying graphic design and plans to make graphic work, art, photography, cooking, travel, and even possibly music his way of life. He has a lot to learn still, and with the help of Ms. Hillary, he feels he will learn what he needs to and more. Many things come to mind when he thinks of the organization: opportunity, safety, hope, and ultimately, freedom. He feels the program gives youth a chance in this world. To him, the program is a blessing and will help him and others gain skills to cope with the world and to turn their minds from becoming self-crippling towards accomplishing their dreams.

From Being Misunderstood to Becoming a Success Story

Another mentee of Ms. Hillary's Kids named Michael Vargas had begun battling depression during Grade 7 and by the time he graduated from high school, he had been hospitalized seven times due to self-mutilation. Up until this point, society and the medical system had been quick to diagnose, label and stereotype Michael. Also quick to prescribe antidepressants, many failed to realize that Michael was simply a misunderstood child whose challenges partly stemmed from an absent alcoholic father, struggling single mother, and having an overly inquisitive nature compared to his peers.

Through the help of Ms. Hillary's Kids mentoring program Michael overcame his challenges. Michael discovered that the best cure was through the ability of positively expressing himself and gaining insight into how to create happiness and success in his life. Being part of the organization has given him opportunities to learn valuable life lessons, from finding his purpose, to managing finances, and even becoming a mentor himself. He teaches others to confront adversities head-on in a peaceful, loving manner. The organization has allowed Michael to learn, connect and network with successful entrepreneurs, authors, radio hosts and Harvard professors; all people with intelligent and caring minds. Though many wouldn't have thought it possible, Michael is now off anti-depressants. He is loving life while attending the Harvard Extension School in Cambridge, Massachusetts. He will undoubtedly become the successful writer that he dreams to be and through Ms. Hillary's Kids, will show younger generations how he succeeded.

As Napoleon Hill once stated, "Whatever your mind can conceive and believe, your mind can achieve." I believe our youth can overcome any obstacle if they put their minds to it and believe!

Bio

Ms. Hillary Vargas is a life coach, motivational speaker, entrepreneur, youth mentor and educator. She is the founder of *Ms. Hillary's Kids*, a non-profit organization designed to support and empower young adults with learning disabilities, behavior challenges or who come from rough or underprivileged backgrounds, as they reach their full and highest potential. She aids them in seeking out the richest soil they can find and planting the seed of their dreams. As they care for the seed with Ms. Hillary's guidance, they slowly see it begin to grow. They care for it, and nurture it, until one day it blooms like a rose from a crack in the concrete.

Ms. Hillary has also served as an educator in several urban schools in Rhode Island and New Jersey, teaching and engaging teenage students in a myriad of topics. Her true passions are teaching and mentoring, and investing in our youth as they are the seeds of our future. She has a BA in Marketing and a minor in Psychology from Johnson & Wales University. As Mahatma Gandhi once eloquently said, "Be the change you wish to see in the world", and Hillary Vargas endeavors to change the world through her students and each person she encounters, one at a time. If you would like to get more information please visit www. mshillaryskids.org or email mshillaryskids@gmail.com.

Ms. Hillary's Kids

Guidance on Success from Today's Experts

Compass Mastermind is a team of Napoleon Hill Foundation Certified Instructors, as well as students taking the Napoleon Hill Foundation certification course.

We come from many countries around the world and, although we speak many languages, we work together, using teamwork and a mastermind alliance, to serve each other and the world.

Our purpose is to serve The Napoleon Hill Foundation, and Napoleon Hill fans from around the world, by helping you to discover, define, and pursue your specific purpose and goals and to encourage you to never give up along the way.

We do that in a number of ways:

- One-on-One Coaching
- Online Mastermind Groups

- Selling Books, Products, and Services from Instructors and Students
- Promoting The Napoleon Hill Foundation Leader Certification course
- Promoting Achievus, the official cooperative board game of The Napoleon Hill Foundation
- Speaking at events
- Attending Napoleon Hill Foundation Leader Certification trips

If there is any way we can help you discover, define, and pursue your goals, please contact us at success@compassmastermind.com

Made in the USA
Charleston, SC
06 January 2016